Primary Mathematics

The PRIMARY MATHEMATICS Team

Barbara Allen, *Author*

Heather Cooke, *Author*

Hilary Evens, *Author*

Alan Graham, *Author*

Eric Love, *Academic Editor*

John Mason, *Author*

Christine Shiu, *Chair and Author*

Gaynor Arrowsmith, *Course Manager*

Sue Dobson, *Graphic Artist*

Sue Glover, *Publishing Editor*

Debra Parsons, *Project Control*

Naz Vohra, *Graphic Designer*

DEVELOPING SUBJECT KNOWLEDGE

PRIMARY MATHEMATICS

HEATHER COOKE

Centre
for
Mathematics
Education

The Open
University

P·C·P

Paul Chapman Publishing Ltd
A SAGE Publications Company
6 Bonhill Street
London EC2A 4PU

SAGE Publications Inc
2455 Teller Road
Thousand Oaks, California 91320

SAGE Publications India Pvt Ltd
32, M-Block Market
Greater Kailash - I
New Delhi 110 048

British Library Cataloguing in Publication data

A catalogue record for this book is available from the British Library

ISBN 0 7619 7117 3
ISBN 0 7619 7118 1 (pbk)

Library of Congress catalog card number available

Typeset by Pantek Arts Ltd
Production by Bill Antrobus, Rosemary Campbell and Susie Home
Printed and bound by Cromwell Press, Trowbridge, Wiltshire

Contents

Preface

The purpose of the Developing Subject Knowledge Series is to provide authoritative distance learning materials on the national requirements for teaching the primary curriculum and achieving Qualified Teacher Status. The series includes key study and audit texts to enable trainees to develop subject knowledge in the three core National Curriculum Subjects of English, mathematics and science up to the standard required for achieving QTS as part of an Initial Teacher Training course. Contributors to this series are all primary practitioners who also work in initial teacher training and have experience of preparing materials for distance learning.

Each book in the series draws on material that will be relevant for all trainees following primary ITT courses in Higher Education Institutions, employment based routes, and graduate study routes. Teachers who completed their training before 1997 will also find these texts useful for updating their knowledge. The series will be of interest to an international audience concerned with primary schooling.

Primary Mathematics is written specifically for initial teacher trainees and practising teachers who need to develop their mathematics subject knowledge and understanding.

The task-driven text emphasizes strategies and processes and is very different from the usual style of mathematics textbooks. It is written with the needs of the under-confident in mind with a strong emphasis on active learning. Common mathematical misconceptions are explored. The book includes a self-assessment section with guidance on how to target study effectively.

Hilary Burgess
Series Editor

Companion books in this series are:

Primary Science by Jane Devereux.

Primary English by Ian Eyres.

Using this book

Primary Mathematics is designed for self-study. Its aim is to help you to enhance and consolidate your existing understanding of a range of mathematical topics and to tackle new mathematical ideas both within the pack itself and in the future. Many people, even those who have successfully passed mathematics examinations in school, lack confidence in their own knowledge and their ability to solve mathematical problems. Revisiting ideas from a slightly different angle and working on them from an adult perspective can reduce anxiety and enable you to move forward with increasing confidence and enjoyment.

Each of the seven main content sections is designed to stand alone and so they can be studied in any order. However we do advise that you start with the section entitled *Learning and doing* as this contains some important advice about strategies for working on mathematical ideas which are applicable to all the other sections. Similarly *Proof and reasoning* draws together threads from several of the other sections, and for many people will be an appropriate way of rounding off their work on this book. Some important mathematical ideas crop up in more than one section. These are cross-referenced in margin notes to allow you to pursue connections useful to your learning.

A list of contents is given on page v.

Two sections are different in nature from the main content ones. The first of these contains *Practice exercises* which provide extra experience in using ideas and techniques introduced throughout the book, in order to improve fluency and consolidate mathematical knowledge. The second is both an index and a guide to creating a personal *Mathematical dictionary*. The index gives page references for important ideas including all those that are printed in bold type in the main text. In the *Mathematical dictionary* you can enter unfamiliar technical terms and their definitions, possibly expressed in your own words to capture your own understanding of them for future reference.

This symbol appears in the margin from time to time to point you to practice exercises on the current topic.

You will also need to use a *calculator* from time to time. The book assumes you are most likely to have a scientific calculator (the kind required for GCSE study) for regular use, but that some readers will possibly own a graphics calculator (with a larger screen which displays each key press). It will also be useful to have occasional access to a four-function calculator (the kind used in primary schools) to compare its handling of calculations with the way your regular scientific or graphics calculator does them.

This symbol appears in the margin when a calculator is needed.

This symbol appears in the margin when the use of a computer would enrich your study.

Access to a *computer* will also enhance your study of mathematics. Any current computer will have a *spreadsheet* (which is a convenient device for doing repeated calculations) as standard, and *dynamic geometry* packages (which allow you to construct and transform geometrical shapes) are readily available. Indications of when these might be useful are given in the text. For those with access to the internet, there is a web page giving supplementary sources of information and useful links. The web address is:

http://mcs.open.ac.uk/cme/passport

Most of this book was previously available as *Passport to Mathematics*. In this new edition there is a *Guide to Assessing Your Subject Knowledge and Understanding*. It is designed in two sections: a section to help you identify any areas of mathematical weakness with the solutions cross-referred to the main text; and a section with practice questions testing your ability to apply your knowledge and understanding. It is suggested that you use this Guide to help you make effective use of the main text.

1. Learning and doing

Introduction

The starting point for learning mathematics is the mathematics the learner can do already. Most of us can carry out calculations when the results are important, for example to decide whether we can save up enough money in time to pay for a longed-for but expensive holiday or whether the football team we support is in danger of relegation. We also use very sophisticated geometrical ideas: we can recognize the three-dimensional reality from two-dimensional objects such as photographs or assembly instructions for a bookcase. This section aims to help you recognize the mathematical know-how you already possess and to teach you some strategies that will enable you to build on it. This will be done by asking you to work on a sequence of tasks. As you read and work on the tasks it will probably be helpful to cover up the text that follows them, including any direct comment on the activity.

For more on calculations see *Number and measure*. For more on 2D and 3D shapes and representations see *Geometry and algebra*.

Average knowledge	Task 1

Think about what you know and understand about the mathematical idea of *average*, and if possible identify some aspect of this that you need to know more about. Try jotting your thoughts down on paper.

It is always worth having pen (or pencil) and paper to hand when working on mathematics.

Comment

Your notes on your thoughts may have gone something like this:

> *What I know* – I remember learning how to find to find the average height of people in my class by adding all the heights together and dividing by the number of people. Later I was told that this kind of average is called a mean and that there are two other kinds of average (at least!), one called mode and one called median.

> *What I want to know* – What are median and mode? Why do I need them? How do I work them out?

You can learn more about the three kinds of average in *Statistics and measuring*, pages 60–62.

If this resembles your own train of thought you have discovered a good working knowledge of 'mean' and are well placed to think about 'median' and 'mode'.

There are strategies which can help you build up your mathematical knowledge. A useful starting point for effective learning is **reviewing** what you know and what you want to know. One powerful way of working on mathematical problems is by setting out ideas and information under the two headings **'I know'** and **'I want'**. After reviewing, **extending** mathematical ideas is a key step. The above example illustrates how many learners begin to extend their early ideas of what is meant by 'average'.

The mathematical ideas in this paragraph are dealt with further in the section *Number and measure*.

Throughout history, mathematical ideas have been extended to new objects – often with much struggle before they were accepted. That your own learning to some extent follows the same paths can be illustrated by the development of numbers. The simplest, most basic numbers are the whole numbers and you learned to add and multiply them. When the number system was extended to fractions, there was a problem of how to extend the operations of addition and multiplication. It was necessary to think about what adding and multiplying fractions meant, how they related to adding and multiplying whole numbers and how these operations could be accomplished. In a similar fashion you may have been puzzled by the extension to negative numbers and the meaning of adding and multiplying them.

Reviewing knowledge, analysing information into 'I know' and 'I want', and extending ideas are all important aspects of mathematical thinking which aid the learning and doing of mathematics. The rest of this section introduces several other aspects of mathematical thinking which can be used as deliberate strategies by learners when trying to make sense of mathematics. Tasks 2 to 8 are related to a single example which lies in the area of number and algebra, though the strategies are just as applicable to other branches of mathematics. Algebra has been chosen because this is often the part of mathematics that causes most anxiety in learners, with the use of letters seeming mysterious and arbitrary. In acknowledgement of this, the example is one which needs the use of only one letter, namely n (standing for any number), and yet demonstrates just how useful that letter can be.

Don't worry if you feel stuck or confused after Task 2. Just continue with Tasks 3 to 8 which are designed to help with sense-making.

Making sense of mathematics

In mathematics, statements can be very condensed so that even a very short statement can carry a lot of meaning and therefore seem difficult to understand at first reading. A first step may be to sort out what you understand by the words and symbols which make up the statement, and then to try to put them together.

Task 2	Sum odd numbers

Read the following statement carefully.

> The sum of the first n odd numbers is equal to n-squared.

What do you understand about what it is saying?

Comment

Your first thoughts may have been to look at words and phrases which make up the statement. If you had jotted them down they might have gone something like this.

> 'The sum of' signals that some things are to be added together.

> In fact 'the first n odd numbers' are to be added. What does that mean?

The odd numbers written in order are:

1, 3, 5, 7, 9, 11, 13, 15, 17, 19, ... and so on.

So the first three odd numbers are 1, 3, 5 and the first four odd numbers are 1, 3, 5, 7. 'n' seems to tell us how many odd numbers to take but it is impossible to write them down as a complete list unless we know what n is!

However, the statement claims that however many n is (whether its value is known or not), then when the first n odd numbers are added up, the answer is n-squared.

And n-squared means $n \times n$ which is usually abbreviated to n^2.

Having sorted out what a statement means may still leave you unsure whether or not it is true. Pause to consider whether you *believe* that it is true that:

The sum of the first n odd numbers is equal to n-squared.

A general statement in mathematics which has not yet been shown to be true, but which someone believes might be true, is called a **conjecture**.

One way of thinking about this is to look at some particular cases. This process is called **specializing**.

In later sections you will do some **conjecturing**.

Try some values	Task 3

Try some particular values of n to see whether the statement is true in those cases.

Comment

There are many possible values you could have tried but it often pays to start with quite small ones. So, for example, you might have tried $n = 3$ and $n = 4$.

$n = 3$:
  The sum of the first three odd numbers is $1 + 3 + 5 = 9$,
  and $n^2 = 3 \times 3 = 9$.

$n = 4$:
  The sum of the first four odd numbers is $1 + 3 + 5 + 7 = 16$,
  and $n^2 = 4 \times 4 = 16$.

When you specialize you are producing your own examples. Being able to do that is an important way of realizing how much you understand.

The statement is certainly true for the cases $n = 3$ and $n = 4$, so it is possible that it is a true statement. A few more values might be even more convincing. So, for example,

$n = 7$:
  The sum of the first seven odd numbers is
  $1 + 3 + 5 + 7 + 9 + 11 + 13 = 49$,
  and $n^2 = 7 \times 7 = 49$.

However, we cannot try out every possible value of n, so we need to find some way of dealing with the situation in general.

Sometimes specializing systematically and recording the results can help in seeing how a pattern continues. Arranging the information above as a table and filling in the intermediate values gives this:

n	Sum of first n odd numbers	n-squared
1	$1 = 1$	$1 \times 1 = 1$
2	$1 + 3 = 4$	$2 \times 2 = 4$
3	$1 + 3 + 5 = 9$	$3 \times 3 = 9$
4	$1 + 3 + 5 + 7 = 16$	$4 \times 4 = 16$
5	$1 + 3 + 5 + 7 + 9 = 25$	$5 \times 5 = 25$
6	$1 + 3 + 5 + 7 + 9 + 11 = 36$	$6 \times 6 = 36$
7	$1 + 3 + 5 + 7 + 9 + 11 + 13 = 49$	$7 \times 7 = 49$

Perhaps the middle column helps you to see how the sum grows by adding on the next odd number to the previous square number.

In fact, one way of gaining insight into why a statement might be true is to use the process of **visualizing**. The next task offers you a visual way of representing what happens when the odd numbers are added together.

Task 4 Picture this

Look at the diagrams below. Think about how they relate to the entries in the table.

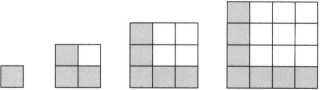

Comment

Perhaps it is inappropriate to describe the diagrams in words at this stage – what you see is what matters. Just reflect briefly on whether the diagrams help to convince you that the statement might be true in general. Are you sure that an odd number is being added on each time?

Visualizing a situation is one way of **using mental imagery**. When mental images take the form of pictures it may not be easy or helpful to try to draw them – they may work much better inside your head. You can demonstrate this for yourself by imagining a small circle rolling round the outside of a bigger circle – and then try drawing what you have imagined.

Imagery need not be visual. Some people find sound an important facet of their powers of imagery – which may be why counting in twos, or fives, or tens can become very rhythmic – and why mistakes can be made when the rhythm is broken for some reason. Also reading out loud is a technique which is often useful in making sense of written mathematics.

Try reading aloud the original claim –

the sum of the first *n* odd numbers is equal to *n*-squared

– to see if hearing the statement makes its meaning any clearer.

Undoing what you did	Task 5

The diagrams in Task 4 showed the building up of a square by adding on odd numbers of small squares. This building up can be described as a mathematical 'doing'. Now try to visualize the next size square and mentally break it down into the L-shaped pieces which formed it. This can be thought of as 'undoing' the building of a square.

Comment

In Task 7 you will be asked to use these L-shaped pictures of odd numbers as a step towards writing down the *n*th odd number.

Very often one mathematical process has the effect of undoing another, so that for example subtraction undoes addition. Although undoing is often harder than the original doing, thinking in terms of **doing and undoing** can be very useful in understanding a situation better.

Awareness of the possibility of undoing a mathematical action also allows new questions to be asked and answered, as in the next task.

Undoing squaring	Task 6

Assuming for the moment that it is certain that the sum of the first *n* odd numbers does equal *n*-squared, is it possible to decide how many odd numbers were added to give the total 121? What is your answer to this?

Comment

Here the 'doing' was squaring and the 'undoing' is finding the square root, in other words finding out what number was multiplied by itself to give 121.

Perhaps you know that 121 is 11-squared, but what if the sum was 361?

Unless you happen to know the square root of 361, the sensible way of

finding it is to use the $\boxed{\sqrt{}}$ key on a calculator. (The square root of 361 is 19.)

Advice on calculator use is given in *Number and measure*, pages 27–30.

Odd numbers in general	Task 7

Recall the L-shaped diagrams for odd numbers. Each one can be thought of as made up of two equal 'branches' and one extra 'corner'. How can this fact be used to write down an expression for the *n*th odd number?

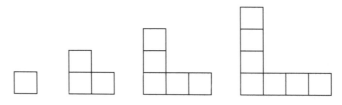

Hint: the first odd number doesn't seem to have any branches so it might be easier to start from the second one.

Comment

The 2nd odd number (3) has branch length 1,   so it equals $1 + 1 + 1 = 2 \times 1 + 1$.

The 3rd odd number (5) has branch length 2,   so it equals $2 + 2 + 1 = 2 \times 2 + 1$.

The 4th odd number (7) has branch length 3,   so it equals $3 + 3 + 1 = 2 \times 3 + 1$.

and so on

Continuing this pattern suggests that

The *n*th odd number has branch length 'one less than *n*', so it equals $2 \times (n - 1) + 1$.

Now $(n - 1) + (n - 1) + 1 = n - 1 + n - 1 + 1 = n + n - 1 = 2n - 1$.

Finally, you might want to make sure that this expression works for the first odd number because that was missed out when the pattern was examined.

In fact, if $n = 1$, then $2n - 1 = 2 \times 1 - 1 = 1$, as required.

Using the L-diagrams to get a formula for the odd numbers is only one of several possible methods. Some people prefer to think in terms of numbers rather than diagrams. A different method, using numbers, is to think first of the even numbers: 2, 4, 6, 8, 10, 12 and so on. It is perhaps fairly easy to see that

$2 = 2 \times 1, \ 4 = 2 \times 2, \ 6 = 2 \times 3, \ 8 = 2 \times 4$

and so, by generalizing, the *n*th even number is *2n*.

Observing that the first odd number (1) is one less than the first even number (2), the second odd number (3) is one less than the second even number (4), and so on, leads to the generalization that the *n*th odd number is one less than *2n*, so it must be $2n - 1$.

The conjecture about adding odd numbers was tested for special cases by using arithmetic. Now, with an algebraic way of writing down the *n*th odd number, it is possible to use algebra in **reasoning** about the sum of *n* odd numbers for any value of *n*.

Even though there is a way of writing the *n*th odd number, since *n* is not known there is no way of writing down *all* the numbers to be added. A way of tackling this is to return to a case where the whole sum *can* be written down to see if that can be generalized.

The table on page 4 went as far as seven odd numbers, so taking $n = 8$, write

SUM (8 odds) = $1 + 3 + 5 + 7 + 9 + 11 + 13 + 15$

One fact which is well known about adding numbers is that it doesn't matter in which order you add them, the same numbers give the same total. So it is equally valid to write

SUM (8 odds) = $15 + 13 + 11 + 9 + 7 + 5 + 3 + 1$

Looking at these two ways of writing the sum can help in seeing links between the numbers which are being added.

SUM (8 odds) $= 1 + 3 + 5 + \ldots + 11 + 13 + 15$

SUM (8 odds) $= 15 + 13 + 11 + \ldots + 5 + 3 + 1$

So

$2 \times$ SUM (8 odds) $= 16 + 16 + 16 + \ldots + 16 + 16 + 16$

$= 8 \times 16$

$= 2 \times 8 \times 8$

and

SUM (8 odds) $= 8 \times 8$

Alternatively you may be able to look at one version of the sum and visualize pairing the first and last numbers (1 and 15), then the second and second last (2 and 14), etc. This way four pairs of numbers each totalling 16 are obtained.

The next step is to see whether this same approach for working out the sum can be made to work for n odd numbers.

SUM (n odds) $= 1 + 3 + 5 + \ldots + (2n - 5) + (2n - 3) + (2n - 1)$

SUM (n odds) $= (2n - 1) + (2n - 3) + (2n - 5) + \ldots + 5 + 3 + 1$

So

$2 \times$ SUM (n odds) $= 2n + 2n + 2n + \ldots + 2n + 2n + 2n$

$= n \times 2n$

$= 2 \times n \times n$

and so

SUM (n odds) $= n \times n = n^2$

At this stage just see if you can follow the reasoning. In particular make sure that you can see why $(2n - 3)$ is the odd number before $(2n - 1)$. Also why if $2 \times$ SUM $= 8 \times 16$ then SUM $= 8 \times 8$.

Only connect   Task 8

You have been asked to look at the same mathematical statement from a lot of different points of view, using at different times arithmetic, algebra and visualizing. Think back to see if you noticed yourself gaining new insight into what was being talked about or made new connections between ideas you had thought of as quite separate.

Comment

Insights – The early calculations and diagrams may have been helpful in illustrating the statement which was being examined. The use of algebra sought to recast the insights from arithmetic and imagery in a form which allows new connections to be made.

Connections – There is good evidence to suggest that mathematical knowledge is at its most secure and usable when the ideas are connected in the mind of the learner. So **making connections** is yet another important mathematical process in learning and doing mathematics.

This section has introduced a number of words and phrases for aspects of mathematical thinking which were signalled by highlighting them in bold. These words –

> reviewing, 'I know' and 'I want', extending, conjecture/conjecturing, specializing, using mental imagery/visualizing, doing and undoing, generalizing, reasoning, making connections

– could be the first entries in your *Mathematical dictionary*. It may be helpful to look at this section now and plan how you will use it.

You may not want to enter the words in the order they appeared, but to arrange them to reflect connections between them. For example, *specializing* (which can be used to look at special cases to help make sense of a generalization) and *generalizing* (forming a generalization on the evidence of particular cases) might be put together or next to each other. Similarly *reviewing* and *extending* are closely linked, as are *reasoning* and *conjecturing*.

Furthermore you may wish to leave space after each entry to add to them when new aspects or insights occur. Even in this section the notions of doing and undoing have been used both to analyse a diagram (Task 4) and to undo a calculation (Task 5).

Notice that almost all the words in the list end in 'ing'. This is because making sense of mathematics is an active process which involves you in doing things. Try to capture that sense of action/activity in your personal definitions in your *Mathematical dictionary*.

In this section you have been asked to use a variety of mathematical processes to aid you in learning and doing mathematics. The final task in this section is a challenge for you to try to use them yourself in making sense of another mathematical claim.

Task 9	Sum challenge

Examine the following statement.

> The sum of the first n counting numbers is equal to half of the sum of n-squared and n.

See if you can sort out what the claim means. If so, decide whether or not you think it is true and how you might explain your insights to someone else.

Comment

Again do as much as you can but don't worry if you get stuck before you are fully satisfied with your response. This mathematical claim is examined in *Proof and reasoning*.

---

2. Number and measure

Introduction

This section is concerned with numbers and their uses. It concentrates on using numbers as measures and for calculating. The issues raised include the following.

- What is the difference between counting and measuring?
- What different kinds of number are there and how are they connected?
- What are the different ways of representing numbers?
- What are efficient methods of calculating, whether using mental methods, calculators or written methods?
- What are the issues involved in calculating with fractions?
- What is involved in measuring?

The section is subdivided into five parts:

- How numbers are used
- Types of number
- Representing numbers
- Calculating
- Measures

Although the parts follow on from each other you may find that what you know already enables you to work through them independently.

How numbers are used

Numbers are used so commonly and in such diverse ways that we often do not notice their presence. Thinking about how and why numbers are used raises some interesting questions, including the following:

- Which objects or situations are worth numbering and why?
- How do numbers arise?
- What sorts of possible numbers are there?
- What is done with numbers?

Having an appreciation of the answers to such questions can assist you in working with numbers.

Your days are numbered?	Task 1

Think back over the last few days and try to recollect how and where you have seen numbers used. What numbers did you come across and in what contexts? What types of number did you encounter?

Comment

Some examples you may have thought of are shown below.

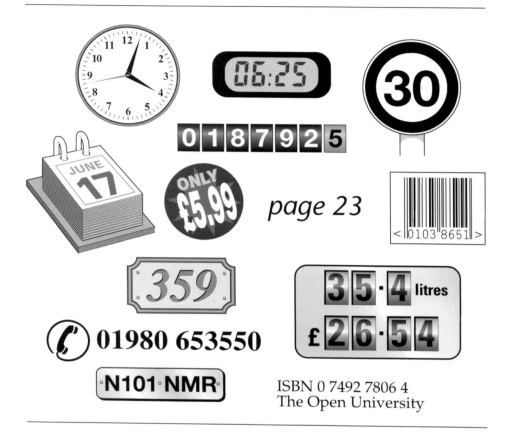

Counting and **measuring** are the two fundamental ways by which humans have introduced numbers into the world. Counting is used when you need to know how many objects there are, whereas measuring is used when the question 'how much?' is asked. A third use of numbers is for **labelling**. Objects are often labelled as a result of counting or measuring, but numbers can be used simply as a label that has no special significance other than to identify something.

Task 2	Sorting

Look at the examples of ways numbers have been used in Task 1 (look at your own examples and those in the diagram). Sort them into three categories depending on whether they have arisen from counting, measuring or labelling. Add any comment about the particular use of numbers in that context.

Comment

One way the examples of numbers can be sorted depends on their different types of use. This process of sorting and categorizing is called **classifying**.

The table below gives four examples.

Example	Purpose	Comment
house number	labelling	odd and even often give information about position
speed limit sign	measuring	units (mph) are omitted
phone number	labelling	can give information about the area
page number	counting	sequence gives information about position

Counting

A count is the number of times something has occurred. When the word 'counting' is used you probably think of numbering objects or events 1, 2, 3, 4, … . If you have ever counted a lot of objects you will know how easy it is to lose your place, or forget your last number. To avoid this happening people resort to using a **tally**, a device where one is added to a total automatically (for example, every time a button is pressed or someone walks through a turnstile). Today, much counting is carried out automatically by such tallies: the word count on a word-processor and the total of cars within a pay car-park are examples.

You might find this when doing a word count for a handwritten essay.

The tally may also be marks on paper, where every fifth mark is drawn across the previous four. This makes totalling relatively easy as the tallies can be counted in fives. This and similar methods then require the total to be calculated when the counting has ended.

The purpose of counting is normally to attach a number in order to be able to compare the size of different sets of objects or events. For example, the unemployment or road accident figures can be compared with those from previous years. Sometimes the total produced by counting may be compared with a known value. In the car-park the total will be compared with the total number of spaces; similarly a blood count can be compared with the expected range of values.

The instance of the unemployment statistics is a reminder that there are considerable problems concerning what is to be counted and how to do it accurately.

As well as being used to compare the relative sizes of sets of objects or events, counting is also used to decide whether a set of things is complete or all there. However, there are occasions when it is not necessary to count every object. For example, many schools have specially designed racks for scissors, calculators and other tools to enable the teacher to see at a glance whether they are all back in place. There is a **one-to-one correspondence** between the tools in the set and the number of spaces in the rack.

Counting produces an exact answer, a whole number. For example, there is a definite number of pages in any book, or cars in a car-park. It is this which distinguishes counting from measuring.

Measuring

When we measure something we are asking the question 'how much?' – how tall, how many, how old, how long something or someone is. So we are now no longer restricted to the counting numbers, but fractions and decimals are possible outcomes (I can be *any* height within a given range). Here we have made a shift from the **discrete** whole numbers to the **continuous** scales of measure.

There is further discussion of the discrete/continuous distinction in *Statistics and measuring*.

Theoretically it is possible for any measurement to be obtained but in practice there are limitations of accuracy due to both the instrument and the measurer.

Much practical measurement takes place without measuring instruments. People decide how long a thread they need to sew on a button, how much salt to put in with the potatoes, whether there is a big enough gap for their car to get past an obstacle, and a host of other everyday tasks without using instruments. This is often called 'estimation', but it is best described as 'informal measuring', or 'measuring without instruments' (it is sometimes called 'measuring by eye'). Slightly more precisely, people use objects which are to hand to compare lengths or weights (a stride, their forearm, a piece of string, a bag of sugar). Then there is measuring in which instruments (tape measures, protractors, weighing scales, etc.) are used.

It is not estimation in the sense of 'estimating a value' or finding an approximate answer.

Task 3   Measuring

Think back to measuring you have done in the last few weeks. Try to list two or three examples each of:

▶ measuring without instruments;

▶ measuring using other objects;

▶ measuring with instruments.

In each case say what and why you measured, and give the instrument when used. Did you use standard units? To what accuracy did you measure?

Comment

Your answers to this question are specific to you and your situation. For example, you might have responded with something like:

> I need a new roller-blind in the bathroom so I measured the height and width of the window recess. I used a tape measure (measuring instrument) marked in centimetres (units used) and rounded up the reading to the nearest centimetre (making decisions about the accuracy required).

Measuring seems essentially a practical activity – measures are found for things in the real world – but when instruments and hence units are involved, measuring has mathematical aspects. These aspects include different systems of units, the relationships between units, and converting between units.

These are dealt with on pages 40–52.

Numbers are needed for both counting and measuring. Whereas counting normally requires whole numbers, measuring also uses fractions and decimals. The relationship between different kinds of number is discussed in the next section.

Types of number

This section looks at the different types of number, the names given to them and the relationships between them.

Numb and number | **Task 4**

How many different types of number on this list do you already know? Could you explain them to someone else or give an example of their use?

counting numbers   integers   decimals
rational numbers   irrational numbers   real numbers
natural numbers   whole numbers   fractions
positive numbers   negative numbers   complex numbers

Comment

It is possible that you can explain some of these types of number but are not sure how they link together. Historically, it took many centuries to invent and then to sort out the different kinds of number – fractions, zero, negative, irrational and so on.

The counting numbers

The smallest counting number is usually taken to be 1. One way to visualize the counting numbers is to imagine a blank line with the counting numbers as stepping stones starting with 1 and going on for ever. The number line below shows the steps going to the right.

1	2	3	4	5	6	7	8	etc.
●	●	●	●	●	●	●	●	…

Since 1 can be added to any number, potentially the counting numbers go on for ever. Counting in English words can eventually run into difficulty, requiring words like *billion, trillion, quadrillion, quintillion,* and so on. With written numbers, however, the principle of place value (together with the number symbols 0–9) is completely versatile: using these digits in combination *any* counting number can be written down.

A billion is usually a thousand million – 'usually' because that was originally the usage in the USA, whereas in Britain it was a million million: the older sense is sometimes still intended.

Other names that are sometimes used for the counting numbers are the **natural numbers** and the **whole numbers**. Both of these uses can be confusing, partly because it is not always clear whether the number zero (or 'nought') is included or not. It is probably best to use 'natural numbers' as an alternative to 'counting numbers', and use 'whole numbers' when you want to include zero.

Task 5	Extending

Another way of thinking of the counting numbers is that they are the ones which can be produced on a calculator just using the keys marked **1, 2, ..., 8, 9** and the $\boxed{+}$ and $\boxed{=}$ keys. What other numbers can you produce using the $\boxed{-}$ key instead of the $\boxed{+}$ key? Where would the numbers go on your number line?

Comment
Using the subtraction key leads to zero and negative numbers.

The integers

The set of **integers** (which are also sometimes referred to, ambiguously, as the whole numbers) comprises zero and the counting numbers (this time thought of as the **positive whole numbers**), and also the **negative whole numbers** ($^-1$, $^-2$, $^-3$, ...). A helpful image here is to picture a mirror placed at the zero of the whole numbers; the negative integers are then the mirror images of the corresponding positive integers.

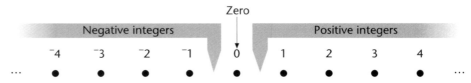

Decimals, fractions and rational numbers

The counting numbers were extended to the integers by using subtraction. Similarly, the counting numbers can be further extended using division. For example:

What number is produced by carrying out the divsion $3 \div 5$?

Three possible answers are:

   $3 \div 5$ gives the decimal 0.6;
   $3 \div 5$ gives the fraction $\frac{3}{5}$;
   $3 \div 5$ gives the rational number $\frac{3}{5}$.

These three answers all represent the same number. **Fractions**, also called **rational numbers**, are an attempt to make the number line like a continuous line rather than a series of stepping stones. On the number line $\frac{3}{5}$ will go between 0 and 1. The decimal 0.6 is a different way of representing the same number.

The rational number $\frac{3}{5}$ arose from the division 3 ÷ 5, but this is not the only division that gives this number.

The word 'rational' comes from **ratio**, which involves expressing the relationship between two numbers.

More divisions   Task 6

Write down several more divisions that will give the answer 0.6. Think how you might generate an unlimited number of such divisions.

Comment

Some possible answers are:

$$6 \div 10,\ 12 \div 20,\ 30 \div 50,\ 12\,000 \div 20\,000$$

It is worth thinking about methods for creating divisions to give the same answer. The answers above suggest some methods. Can you use them to create more divisions? Can you produce a division that is unlikely to be produced by anyone else?

Each of the fractions created from the divisions given in Task 6,

$$\frac{6}{10},\ \frac{12}{20},\ \frac{30}{50},\ \frac{12\,000}{20\,000},$$

represent the same rational number, the same point on the number line. They are called **equivalent fractions** and the underlying number is called the rational number. When you name a rational number it is usual to give either the decimal or the fraction involving the smallest numbers – in this case, 0.6 or $\frac{3}{5}$. The choice between using fractions or decimals depends on the need to make a calculation easier or to make communication clearer. When using a calculator it is likely that using decimals is more efficient.

Fractions and decimals are not different types of number, but different ways of representing rational numbers.

Dividing any whole number by another gives a rational number. For example, starting with 1 and 2, dividing 1 by 2 gives $\frac{1}{2}$, a new point on the number line that is equidistant between 0 and 1. Of course, the division could be performed the other way round: 2 divided by 1 gives the result 2 ($\frac{2}{1} = 2$) which is a whole number. This demonstrates that the integers can also be thought of as rational numbers, since they can be produced by dividing two whole numbers – themselves and 1.

$\frac{2}{1}$ is the reciprocal of $\frac{1}{2}$.

Dividing one integer by another appears to produce a system of numbers which fills every possible point on the number line. For example, 2.1 and 2.2 can be obtained as $\frac{21}{10}$ and $\frac{22}{10}$ respectively; and it is possible to think of a rational number lying between them: 2.13 or 2.17, perhaps. This can be achieved by dividing by 100 instead of 10:

$$\frac{213}{100} = 2.13 \text{ and } \frac{217}{100} = 2.17$$

By a similar process, a rational number between 2.13 and 2.14 can be found by choosing 1000 as the divisor:

$$\frac{2136}{1000} = 2.136$$

This process can be carried out between any pair of decimals.

Task 7	Filling the gaps

Create numbers between 4.1722 and 4.1723 and between 4.1729 and 4.173. Try to imagine the numbers on your number line.

Comment

Between the two adjacent numbers 4.1722 and 4.1723 nine new numbers can be fitted by this process: 4.172 21, 4.172 22, 4.172 23, ..., 4.172 29. The process is completely general. On a number line composed of rational numbers, the gap between any two numbers can be filled with more rational numbers by increasing the divisor by a multiple of 10.

Here is a number line with some rational numbers.

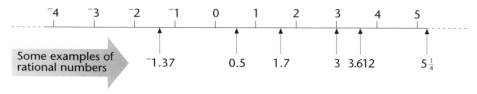

Ordering fractions and decimals

It is often convenient to express fractions as decimals since ordering fractions can be quite difficult. For example, not many people could say immediately which of $\frac{8}{11}$ and $\frac{7}{9}$ is the larger. Decimals, because they use the place-value system, can be ordered in size more readily, but there are features of ordering decimals that many school pupils find confusing. You may have fallen into some of these traps yourself in the past. See if you recognize the possible confusions in the following task.

Task 8	Ordering decimals

Write the following decimals in order, smallest first:

(a) 0.07, 0.23, 0.1

(b) 0.735, 0.74

(c) ⁻3.75, ⁻2.84

In each case give a reason why a school pupil might give the wrong answer.

Comment

(a) 0.07, 0.1, 0.23 is correct. A pupil might ignore the decimal point and write 0.1, 0.07, 0.23 because they see only the 1, 7 and the 23 and put those in order.

(b) 0.735, 0.74 is correct. A pupil might believe 0.74 is smaller than 0.735 because it contains fewer digits.

(c) ⁻3.75, ⁻2.84 is correct. A pupil might believe that ⁻2.84 is smaller because, with the positive numbers 2.84 and 3.75, 2.84 *is* smaller.

It has been suggested that some of these mistakes may partly be due to the over-emphasis on using money as a means of introducing decimals. For example, £1.25 is said 'one pound twenty-five', whereas 1.25 is said 'one point two five'. A very common error is to say 'one point twenty-five' for the decimal.

Infinite decimals

If you attempted to find which of $\frac{8}{11}$ and $\frac{7}{9}$ is the larger fraction by carrying out the divisions on a calculator, you would get:

$\frac{8}{11} = 0.727\ 272\ 727$ and $\frac{7}{9} = 0.777\ 777\ 778$

(The number of digits shown depends upon your calculator.) In each case the answer is an infinite **recurring** (repeating) **decimal**. All rational numbers produce a decimal which is either terminating or recurring. So, for example:

$\frac{1}{3} = 0.333\ 333\ 333...$, $\frac{41}{333} = 0.123\ 123\ 123\ 123...$ and $\frac{27}{250} = 0.108$

There are also infinite decimals that neither terminate or recur; and which cannot be obtained by dividing two integers. These numbers are called the **irrational numbers** (i.e. the *not-rationals*) and fill the gaps in the number line left between the rational numbers. They include numbers like $\sqrt{2}$ (the number which when multiplied by itself gives 2), $\sqrt{5}$, and so on. Amazingly, the decimal expansion of $\sqrt{2}$ never repeats itself:

> 1.414 213 562 373 095 048 801 688 724 209 698 078 569 671 875 376 948 073 176 679 737 990 732 478 462 107 038 850 387 534 327 641 572 735 013 846 230 912 297 024 924 836 055 850 737 212 644 121 497 099 935 831 413 222 665 927 505 592 755 799 950 501 152 782 060 571 470 109 ... (and on and on ...)

Another irrational number is π. Thus π is not equal to $\frac{22}{7}$ (which is a recurring decimal), but that fraction is a close approximation, though a little smaller than π. An even better approximation (slightly larger than π) is $\frac{355}{113}$.

π can be defined either as the area of a circle whose radius is one unit, or as the ratio of the circumference to the diameter of any circle.

Real numbers

The set of numbers that include the rationals and irrationals are called the **real numbers**. Despite the variety of names, any number can be thought of as a point lying somewhere on the number line.

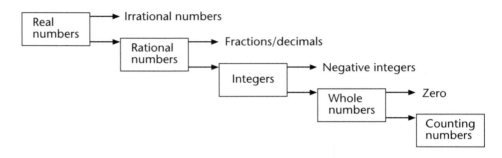

There is yet one more type of number – **complex numbers**. These are based on $\sqrt{-1}$ which has the symbol i. Complex numbers are ones which use both real numbers and i ($2 + 3i$ is an example). Although such numbers can seem strange, they have many practical applications in engineering and science, and are used to create the popular pictures of chaos and fractals. This book does not cover complex numbers but it is worth knowing that such numbers exist.

Representing numbers

The four most common ways of representing numbers you will come across are:

▶ the place-value system (the usual way of representing whole numbers and decimals);

▶ index notation;

▶ scientific notation;

▶ percentage notation.

These are each examined in this section.

The place-value system

The Indian–Arabic (or Hindu–Arabic) system most generally used in the western world has ten numerals (0, 1, 2, 3, 4, 5, 6, 7, 8, 9) which are combined in a place-system structure. The name of the symbol 6 in English is 'six', but the meaning changes depending on its position such as:

six	→	sixty	→	six hundred	→	six thousand
6		60		600		6000

The place-value system is based on powers of ten and of course extends to decimals.

Ten thousands	Thousands	Hundreds	Tens	Units	tenths	hundredths	thousandths
10 000	1000	100	10	1	0.1	0.01	0.001

Index notation

Using power notation for numbers, writing numbers as 5^2, 3^8 and so on, is only a shorthand, but an efficient one. For example, multiplying 5s together successively gives:

$5 \times 5 = 25$ $5 \times 5 \times 5 = 125$ $5 \times 5 \times 5 \times 5 = 625$
$5 \times 5 \times 5 \times 5 \times 5 = 3125$ etc.

Using the shorthand notation this becomes:

$5^2 = 25$ $5^3 = 125$ $5^4 = 625$ $5^5 = 3125$

In this example, 5 is the **base** number and the superscript number at the top right indicates how many of these base numbers have been multiplied together. This superscript number is called the **power** or **index** or **exponent**.

The term 5^5 is read as 'five to the power 5' and 5^4 as 'five to the power 4'. Although 5^3 could be read as 'five to the power 3' it is usually said 'five cubed'; it may help you to remember this by relating it to a cube in 3D space. Similarly 5^2 is usually read as 'five squared' and relates to a square in 2D space.

The powers 2, 3 and 4 in 5^2, 5^3, 5^4 are all counting numbers. However, the value of this shorthand arises when the index number is extended to negative and fractional numbers. The extension to negative numbers is looked at here. The original numbers are:

Index	2	3	4	5
Power of 5	25	125	625	3125

Imagine reading from right to left: the numbers in the top row are going down in 1s, the numbers in the bottom row are being divided by 5. If the top row is extended leftwards the table would read:

$^-3$	$^-2$	$^-1$	0	1	2	3	4	5
$\frac{1}{125}$	$\frac{1}{25}$	$\frac{1}{5}$	1	5	25	125	625	3125

In this process of extending a mathematical idea, the pattern of numbers in the table has been preserved, but where previously we could say that $5^3 = 5 \times 5 \times 5$ was 'three 5s multiplied together', it is not possible to think of 5^{-3} in the same way as 'negative three 5s multiplied together'. Usually, when extending a mathematical idea, some aspects are preserved and others lost.

This extension gives:

$$5^1 = 5 \qquad 5^0 = 1 \qquad 5^{-1} = \tfrac{1}{5} \qquad 5^{-2} = \tfrac{1}{25} \qquad 5^{-3} = \tfrac{1}{125}$$

Notice that:

$$5^{-2} = \frac{1}{5^2} \qquad 5^{-3} = \frac{1}{5^3} \qquad \text{and so on}$$

Of course this notation does not just apply to powers of 5 but to powers of any number. It is especially used with powers of 10 because 10 is the basis for the place-value system.

Thousands	Hundreds	Tens	Units	tenths	hundredths	thousandths
1000	100	10	1	0.1	0.01	0.001
10^3	10^2	10^1	10^0	10^{-1}	10^{-2}	10^{-3}

Scientific notation

A simple ('four-function') calculator will have a display that shows probably eight digits on it. So the largest number that can be entered is 99 999 999, and the smallest is ⁻99 999 999. The number closest to 0 (apart from 0 itself) will be 0.000 000 1. Calculations involving bigger numbers or ones closer to zero need a scientific calculator which shows numbers written in **scientific notation** (also known as **standard form**).

Using this notation, numbers can be expressed in a particularly neat form as illustrated by the following examples:

$$250 \ = 2.5 \times 10^2$$
$$25 \ \ = 2.5 \times 10^1$$
$$2.5 \ \ = 2.5 \times 10^0$$
$$0.25 = 2.5 \times 10^{-1}$$

In general

any number = (number between 1 and 10) × (power of 10)

Note that a scientific calculator:

▸ may possibly display numbers with ten or more digits;

▸ will also display larger (and smaller) numbers using scientific notation.

Task 9   Big numbers

What answer would you expect if you find the square of 20 million (i.e. multiply 20 million by itself)? How many noughts should the answer have?

If you have a scientific calculator available, enter 20 000 000 and then press the 'square' key, usually marked $\boxed{x^2}$.

Comment

You should find that the calculator will display 4.0 14, or perhaps 4.0 E14. (Different calculators may display the answer in various ways.) These both mean:

$$4.0 \times 10^{14}, \text{ or } 400\ 000\ 000\ 000\ 000$$

Try some more calculations which involve the use of huge numbers.

The letter E here stands for 'exponent'.

A scientific calculator will enable you to extend the end of the number line up to something like 9.9999×10^{99}. This is quite a big number, but the space for numbers beyond is still infinitely large! However, most scientific calculators will helpfully display 'ERROR' if you venture into parts of the number line that they are not programmed to reach.

Small numbers very close to zero can also be formed in this way. For example, set up your calculator constant facility to divide by 10, enter a simple starting value, say 43, and then repeatedly press the $\boxed{=}$ key.

Methods of using your calculator constant facility are explained on pages 29–30.

Watch carefully how, after about nine presses, the display suddenly jumps into scientific notation and you see 4.3 ‾08, 4.3 ‾09, ... Extending this principle, the smallest number greater than zero that this calculator can handle will be 1.0 ‾99. There is still a very small gap between this number and zero. However, even within this extremely small region, an infinity of numbers exist!

A version of roughly what the scientific calculator number line might look like is shown below. It assumes a model with only an eight-digit display. To avoid making the diagram look too cluttered, we have separated out the two forms of number – the numbers expressed in conventional notation are shown above the number line and the numbers expressed in scientific notation appear below it.

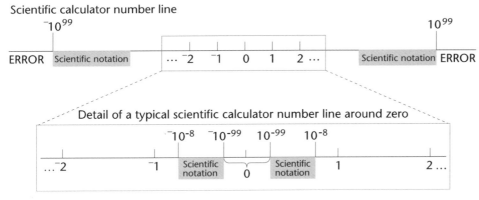

It is worth while spending some time studying this diagram and being quite precise about what the significant boundaries mean and where they lie. For example, can you distinguish between the very large negative number, $^{-}10^{99}$, and the very small positive number, 10^{-99}?

Small and large numbers in practice

In practice you are unlikely to come across many examples of very small numbers except in the context of measurement. A useful small unit of length is a micron (µm) which is a millionth of a metre or 1×10^{-6} m. For example, the diameter of a grain of pollen from the lesser celandine is 33 microns and the diameter of a bacterium is even smaller – somewhere between 1 and 5 microns. In the technological world the distances between the tracks of an ordinary compact disc are about 1.6 µm and in the second generation of CDs, called Digital Versatile Discs (DVDs), the tracks are even closer at 0.74 µm apart – roughly half the distance. This means that the length of spiral available for data is about twice as long, so the DVDs can carry twice as much data.

Note that this is an example of inverse proportion: as the distance between the grooves gets smaller the data spiral gets longer.

This would be a good point to ensure that you know how to enter different types of numbers directly onto your calculator.

Task 10	Entering numbers

Check that you know how to enter different types of number on your calculator:

(a) Negative numbers – can you get your calculator to work out $^-3 \times {}^-5$?

(b) Can you enter and use decimals?

(c) If you have a scientific calculator, do you know how to enter a number such as 9.46×10^{12} (the number of kilometres in one light-year)?

Percentages

Are percentages fractions, decimals, or something else? An extract from a newspaper report on changes in shopping reads:

> Total sales by butchers have slipped in every year of this decade; last year's total of £1.7 billion is 62 per cent of that of 1990. … The top 10 chain [stores] account for half the total sales of all 775 companies in the report and two-fifths of all shop-spending in Britain.

(Source: *Guardian*, 5 May 1998)

This mixture of numbers written as decimals, percentages and fractions is very common in the media; it is useful to be able to relate them easily.

Percentages are often thought of as fractions, so 45% is $\frac{45}{100}$. But because the denominator of the fraction is hundredths, it is usually more appropriate, especially when using a calculator, to think of percentages as decimals in disguise: 45% = 0.45. This means that finding a percentage of something is the same as multiplying by a decimal.

A label that reads '60% cotton and 40% polyester' means that $\frac{60}{100}$, or $\frac{6}{10}$ (0.6), is cotton while $\frac{40}{100}$, or $\frac{4}{10}$ (0.4), is polyester.

Fractions and decimals can both be seen as the result of a division, and so moving from fractions to percentages is best done by changing the fraction to a decimal and then changing the decimal to a percentage.

See page 14.

$$\frac{3}{4} = 0.75 = \frac{75}{100} = 75\%$$

Sometimes it will not be an exact amount.

$$\frac{5}{6} \approx 0.8333 \approx 0.83 = 83\%$$

Calculating

The 'four rules'

The concepts of addition, subtraction, multiplication and division are complex abstract ideas which are interrelated.

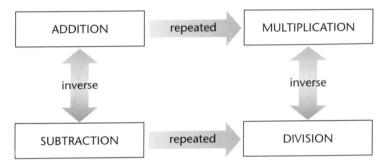

Since concepts are, by definition, abstract, they cannot be expressed precisely in words or diagrams. However, aspects can be illustrated by example.

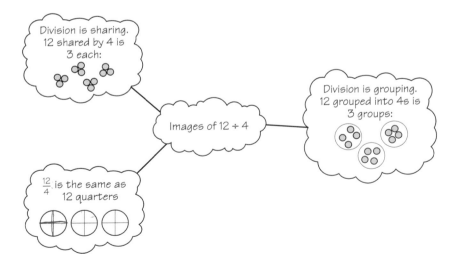

The various ways of doing calculations involving the four rules can be categorized by the different means used:

- mental methods;
- methods using a calculator;
- written methods.

Task 11	Choosing a method

Consider the following calculations:

(a) $361 - 261$ (b) 361×261 (c) $361 + 261$

What method would you use for each of these: mental, written, or a calculator?

Comment

The methods you use will depend on how adept you are at each of them. You may have worked out $361 - 261 = 100$ mentally, whereas it is more likely that you used a calculator to work out $361 \times 261 = 94\ 221$. When working out $361 + 261 = 622$ it is possible that you used any one of the methods or indeed all three. It is quite common for people to use a combination of all three methods.

When you are manipulating numbers you are aiming for fluency as well as accuracy, but not necessarily great speed. There are some skills and strategies that help when using each of these methods.

This section looks at the various methods of calculating – mental methods, ones using a calculator, and written methods. It then discusses calculating with fractions, decimals, percentages and ratios. For such calculations, most people use a mixture of methods depending on the numbers involved.

Mental methods

In recent times there has been a much increased emphasis on mental arithmetic in schools, and most adults sometimes use mental methods for informal calculations where the numbers are simple or a calculator is not to hand. Quick recall of number facts and fast mental calculation has been taken to be evidence of understanding and high mathematical ability. Equally, poor recall and slow calculation has been taken as evidence of low ability. But these are very dubious assertions.

This section helps you think about the methods you use when calculating mentally (you may find that you use more than you are aware of). Useful mental calculating strategies are then looked at.

There are several important aspects to mental calculation:

- For any mental calculation there can be a wide variety of methods – some are more efficient than others for *particular numbers*, while some are more efficient for the *particular person* doing the calculation. Also, there is variation in the need for accuracy, determined by the purpose of the calculation in the context in which it arose.

- There is a need to understand ('have a feel for') numbers and operations in order to *devise* an appropriate method.

- Mental methods commonly take a different form from the standard written methods.

- Mental methods can be shared; they do not need to be re-invented by every individual.

Use the following task as a way of finding out some of the methods you use.

Buying stamps   Task 12

Mentally work out how much it would cost to buy the following postage stamps (do each part without using the solution to a previous one). Think about what method you use.

(a) 50 at 28p each   (b) 27 at 50p each

(c) 25 at 75p   (d) 28 at 75p

Comment

Did you always use the same method? If not, why not? The following are some which you might have used for part (d):

- $75p = £\frac{3}{4}$, $28 \times \frac{3}{4} = 28 \div 4 \times 3 = 7 \times 3 = £21$

- $2 \times 75p = £1.50$, $14 \times 1.50 = (10 \times 1.50) + (4 \times 1.50) = 15 + 6 = £21$

- $20 \times 0.75 = 15$, $8 \times 0.75 = 6$, $15 + 6 = £21$

- 2 stamps cost £1.50 so 4 cost £3; 28 is 7 groups of 4, $7 \times £3 = £21$

Mental strategies

With mental calculations there are no set methods – what you use depends on your personal strategies and the actual numbers. This creates difficulties for some people who feel lost without a standard method to hold on to. However, there is plenty of evidence that you can improve your mental arithmetic by being more aware of strategies you use and deliberately adopting new ones. For example, one strategy is to break down a number into parts that are easier to deal with. This strategy is often used by people who can work out VAT in their heads. At the time of writing VAT is payable at 17.5%. At first glance this appears to be a bizarre amount. But you can break down 17.5% as follows:

$$17.5\% = 10\% + 5\% + 2.5\%$$

You use a **method** with particular numbers, but a **strategy** is more like a generalization of a collection of methods.

To work out 17.5% of £48 you would calculate these three percentages (10% is easy, and the others are each half of the previous one) and add them:

$$17.5\% \text{ of } £48 = £4.80 + £2.40 + £1.20$$
$$= £8.40$$

Try this method on £64.

You may have found that you had difficulty in 'holding' three different figures in your head. Mental methods do not need to be entirely 'in the head'; it is often useful to jot down intermediate numbers.

Here is another example: 506 – 309.

> *Method 1*: Taking 300 from 506 gives 206. Taking 9 from 206 gives 197.

> *Method 2*: Taking 300 from 500 gives 200. Taking 6 from 9 gives 3. Taking 3 from 200 gives 197.

> *Method 3*: Make the 309 up to 400 which gives 91, then add 100, then add the 6, giving 197.

These three methods share a common feature in that they work with the bigger numbers, the hundreds, before the units. In the standard written methods, the rule is to start with the units for addition, subtraction and multiplication, but not for division!

Below are some common strategies that you might use.

Addition and subtraction strategies

- Count on or back in repeated steps of 10, 2 or 5.
- Identify near doubles and adjust.
- Separate into tens and units and add tens first.
- Add/subtract 9, 19, 29, … or 11, 21, 31, … by adding/subtracting 10, 20, 30, … then adjusting by 1.
- Add several small numbers and look for pairs that total 10.

Multiplication and division strategies

- To multiply by 10, shift digits one place to the left.
- To divide by 10, shift digits one place to the right.
- Use the relationship between multiplication and division as inverses.
- Use related facts of doubling and halving.
- Use closely related facts already known.
- Split numbers into parts that are easily dealt with.

Calculators

While it is possible to use calculators for simple calculations, they are not always the most efficient method. For example, the calculation 22 + 23 requires six key presses to get the answer:

2 2 ☐+ **2 3** ☐=

Doing a sum like this mentally is usually faster than using a calculator; you need to use your judgement about when to reach for a calculator.

Many people are sometimes unsure exactly which keys to press to work out a calculation: for example, £12.99 less 5% discount. This is partly because people are often unsure how to use particular kinds of keys, and partly because calculators do not always give the outcome you might expect. This section examines the following issues:

▸ unexpected answers on calculators;

▸ calculator logics;

▸ the use of the calculator constant facility.

The next task draws your attention to some of the features of a calculator operation. The intention is to raise issues through your being surprised, perhaps, at the answers the calculator gives.

Calculator key sequences are shown with the numbers in **bold** and the operation keys in a box.

Guess and press   Task 13

(a) Look at each key sequence below. Before you use the calculator, *write down* what answer you would expect it to produce on the calculator display.

(b) For each key sequence, press the keys in the given order on your calculator and write down the result you actually got. Clear the calculator display before moving to the next key sequence.

(i) **7** ☐÷ **4**   (ii) **3** ☐÷ **4** ☐=   (iii) **2** ☐÷ **3** ☐=

(iv) **2** ☐+ **3** ☐× **4** ☐=   (v) **2** ☐+ ☐+ **3** ☐=

(vi) **2** ☐+ ☐+ **3** ☐= ☐=

Comment

Some examples of the sorts of issues that this task was designed to raise are given below.

(i) **7** ☐÷ **4**

As written, most calculators will show 4. Two points arising from this are, first, that most calculator key sequences require the press of ☐= to complete them, and second, that it is worth clearly distinguishing between a textbook 'sum' and a calculator key sequence.

Although this task can be carried out on your own, it is better done with a small group of people working and discussing together.

Some calculators do not have a ☐= key but have an

☐ENTER key

instead.

(ii) **3** $\div$ **4** $=$ and   (iii) **2** $\div$ **3** $=$

Although the first division (3 ÷ 4) gives an exact answer, the second (2 ÷ 3) produces a string of digits which (in theory) goes on for ever. This reveals two interesting features of your calculator. First, does it 'round' the final digit up to 7, or does it 'cut' the string, leaving a 6 as the final digit displayed? Second, how many digits can your calculator display – eight, ten or twelve?

(iv) **2** $+$ **3** $\times$ **4** $=$

This sequence will produce the answer 14 or 20, depending on the operating system of the calculator you are using. This is an important thing to know and is explained more fully in the next task, 'Calculator logic'.

(v) **2** $+$ $+$ **3** $=$ and   (vi) **2** $+$ $+$ **3** $=$ $=$

These sequences are likely to raise questions about the calculator's constant facility. The constant facility is such a useful feature of calculators that it is also explored later in this section.

One of the problems of working with calculators is that they do not all work in the same way. You have to get to know your particular calculator and its nuances.

Task 14	Calculator logic

Imagine that someone asks you to do the following calculation in your head. Read it out loud before doing it.

> What is 2-plus-3 (pause) times 4?

Now try the following calculation, again reading it out loud first.

> What is 2 plus (pause) 3-times-4?

Finally, here is an exercise in algebra to try.

> Find the value of the expression 2 + 3a, when $a = 4$.

Comment

It is likely that for the first sentence, when read as written above, you will produce the answer 20. For the second calculation, although the basic words are the same, the answer is less certain. If you read the '3-times-4' part all in a rush, as written above, the answer 14 may seem more appropriate (i.e. as 2 + 12).

The algebra example, when the a is replaced by 4, produces the same calculation, namely $2 + 3 \times 4$. This time the answer of 14 is inescapable, because the rules of algebra dictate that the multiplication of 3×4 must be completed before the 2 is added.

So, what will your calculator make of $2 + 3 \times 4$?

Calculators, unfortunately, are not programmed to interpret dramatic pauses and changes of intonation when given instructions to perform a calculation. They will simply calculate according to the rules with which they have been programmed.

Most calculators have either an arithmetic or an algebraic operating system. Calculators which perform the operations from left to right in the order in which they are keyed in (i.e. ones which will give the answer 20 to the above sequence) are said to have an 'arithmetic operating system'. Calculators which conform to algebraic rules, such as that multiplication and division must be performed before addition and subtraction (i.e. which will give the answer 14 to the above sequence) are said to have an 'algebraic operating system'.

This is pronounced arith**met**ic, with the stress on the third syllable.

Most of the calculators found in primary classrooms are often termed 'four-function' machines. These usually have arithmetic logic and will carry out addition, subtraction, multiplication and division of numbers (the four functions referred to in the name). On the other hand, scientific calculators tend to conform to an algebraic operating system.

The calculator constant facility

An especially useful feature of a calculator is the 'constant' facility: the method by which you can carry out repeat operations.

The constant facility is a way of setting up the calculator to do a particular calculation and, thereafter, it will continue to perform the same calculation each time the $=$ key is pressed. The constant facility can be thought of as a form of 'function machine', where you input a number into the calculator, press $=$ to apply the function, and the output value then appears in the display.

The constant facility and the $\boxed{\%}$ key are the two aspects of a simple calculator that many people find the most puzzling.

Setting up the constant facility

Almost all calculators have a constant facility, but unfortunately they do not all operate with the constant in the same way. The two most common methods of setting up and operating the constant, the 'automatic' and the 'double-press' constant, are described below. Check which way works for your machine. If neither works, track down the calculator's manual and see whether it can be set up by some other means (for example, some calculator constants are based on a key marked $\boxed{K}$).

Checking the constant facility   Task 15

This will enable you to check whether your calculator has an automatic or a double-press constant.

(a) Carry out this sequence:

    2 $\boxed{+}$ $\boxed{+}$ $\boxed{=}$ $\boxed{=}$ $\boxed{=}$ ...

For calculators with a double-press constant, this key sequence should produce the 2 times table. (Many calculators show a small 'κ' in the display to indicate that the constant has been activated.) For calculators with an automatic constant, '2' will remain in the display.

(b) Carry out this sequence:

8 $\boxed{+}$ **2** $\boxed{=}$ $\boxed{=}$ $\boxed{=}$ $\boxed{=}$ …

If successive presses of $\boxed{=}$ have the effect of changing the number on the display, then you know that your calculator has an automatic constant facility. Such calculators will produce a sequence of numbers. (Other calculators will show '10' on the display throughout.)

(c) (Only if you have a calculator with an automatic constant.)
There is more than one type of automatic constant. You need to discover whether the constant operation is applied to the number *before* the operation each time (i.e. the **8**) or the number *after* it (the **2**). This needs to be checked out carefully for any new calculator you use, as it varies from model to model. To find out which type you have, carry out the following sequences:

8 $\boxed{-}$ **2** $\boxed{=}$ $\boxed{=}$ $\boxed{=}$ $\boxed{=}$ …

8 $\boxed{\times}$ **2** $\boxed{=}$ $\boxed{=}$ $\boxed{=}$ $\boxed{=}$ …

8 $\boxed{\div}$ **2** $\boxed{=}$ $\boxed{=}$ $\boxed{=}$ $\boxed{=}$ …

Using the constant facility

Below are some key sequences for you to try. They assume the double-press constant. If your calculator constant operates differently, the key sequences will need to be adapted.

(a) Pressing **10** $\boxed{+}$ $\boxed{+}$ **5** $\boxed{=}$ $\boxed{=}$ $\boxed{=}$ $\boxed{=}$ … should give 15, 25, 35, 45, …

(b) Pressing **1** $\boxed{-}$ $\boxed{-}$ **11** $\boxed{=}$ $\boxed{=}$ $\boxed{=}$ $\boxed{=}$ … should give 10, 9, 8, 7, …

This method is used later in converting units of measurement.

The constant facility can be of use to a teacher. Below is a method of converting a set of class results, marked out of a total of 65, into percentages.

Set the adjustment factor: press **100** $\boxed{\div}$ **65** $\boxed{=}$.

Set up the constant: press $\boxed{\times}$ $\boxed{\times}$.

Adjust the first mark: enter mark 1 and press $\boxed{=}$.
(Don't press the 'Clear' key before entering the next mark.)

Adjust the second mark: enter mark 2 and press $\boxed{=}$.
And so on.

One problem with the constant facility is that it is rather fragile, in that it will vanish if any operation key or the 'Clear' key is pressed.

Written methods

Written methods of calculation are useful when:

▶ calculations are too complex to be done entirely mentally, and a calculator is not available;

▶ when the process of calculation needs to be communicated to someone else.

These needs occur much less frequently than they used to. The 'standard written methods' were devised to enable clerks, who had no other aids to calculation, to carry out calculations efficiently. 'Efficiency' involved writing down as little as possible, while still leaving the intermediate calculations apparent and hence available for subsequent checking. Today, the standard written methods are used remarkably little in the adult world. This may be because they are so difficult to learn and remember, but it is more likely because they are seldom the most appropriate to use. You probably find that you use mainly mental methods, informal writing down and the calculator.

These routines for written calculations are referred to as 'standard written methods', 'standard written algorithms', or 'traditional pencil-and-paper methods'. Examples are the 'decomposition' method for subtraction, and the method of 'long multiplication'.

Written methods for the four rules on whole numbers are not discussed here as they are likely to be familiar to you. One of the aspects of whole numbers where you may use a mix of written and calculator methods is in finding their factors.

Finding **multiples** of a number is straightforward. The multiples of 6, say, are just those numbers into which 6 divides exactly: 6, 12, 18, 24, 30, … . They are the numbers in the 6 times table. Undoing the process – finding what numbers divide exactly into a given number; that is, finding the **factors** – is not so easy. In fact, for large numbers it is extremely difficult, which is why it is used as a basis for creating codes that are difficult to break.

It is not obvious what the factors are of, say, 2093. There are actually eight numbers which divide 2093 exactly: 1, 7, 13, 23, 91, 161, 299, 2093. How could you find such numbers? There are two key aspects:

▶ Factors occur in pairs: if 7 divides into 2093 exactly it must pair with another number that also divides into 2093. In fact, $7 \times 299 = 2093$.

▶ Some of the factors are **prime numbers**. The rest are made up of those prime numbers.

There is an infinite number of prime numbers.

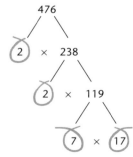

This method is usually called 'producing a factor tree'.

Prime numbers are those that have just two numbers that will divide them: 1 and the number itself. So 2, 3, 5, 7, 11, 13 are all prime numbers. 1 is not a prime number as it only has one divisor.

For 2093, the eight numbers pair as follows:

$1 \times 2093, \ 7 \times 299, \ 13 \times 161, \ 23 \times 91$

The prime numbers here are 7, 13, 23. The other numbers each have other factors:

$91 = 7 \times 13, \ 161 = 7 \times 23, \ 299 = 13 \times 23$

Notice that these factors are each made by multiplying together **prime factors**. This example suggests a method for finding the factors of any number. This is demonstrated in the margin with the number 476.

The factors of 476 that are prime numbers are the ringed ones: 2, 2, 7, 17.
So
$$476 = 2 \times 2 \times 7 \times 17$$

Task 16	Finding the factors

Find the prime factors of:

(a) 72   (b) 855

Comment

The factors are:

(a) $72 = 2 \times 2 \times 2 \times 3 \times 3$

(b) $855 = 3 \times 3 \times 5 \times 19$

Calculating with fractions

When calculations involve fractions you are unlikely to use only written methods. Most people use a mixture of written, mental and calculator methods, depending on the numbers involved.

Task 17	Adding fractions

How would you carry out the following calculation?

$$\tfrac{1}{4} + \tfrac{1}{3}$$

Comment

You were probably taught this method at school:

$$\tfrac{1}{4} + \tfrac{1}{3} = \tfrac{3}{12} + \tfrac{4}{12} = \tfrac{7}{12}$$

For this method you need to use equivalent fractions – which you saw on the number line. To add or subtract fractions each **denominator** (number under the bar) must be the same. So:

$$\tfrac{1}{4} = \tfrac{2}{8} = \tfrac{3}{12} = \ldots \quad \text{and} \quad \tfrac{1}{3} = \tfrac{2}{6} = \tfrac{3}{9} = \tfrac{4}{12} = \ldots$$

Many people find the addition and subtraction of fractions cumbersome. If the question was more complicated then it would make sense to use a calculator that can add fractions, such as a graphics calculator. In reality it is likely that the fractions will be changed to decimals before they are manipulated. But this can introduce an inaccuracy in the calculation when the decimal forms of the numbers are infinite repeating decimals. For example:

$$\tfrac{3}{7} + \tfrac{1}{3} = \tfrac{16}{21}$$

but, in decimals, a four-function calculator gives:

$$0.428\ 571\ 4 + 0.333\ 333\ 3 = 0.761\ 904\ 7$$

The decimal for $\frac{16}{21}$ is 0.761 904 761 904 ... which when rounded to the seventh decimal place differs from the calculator result. This discrepency does not usually matter in practical questions.

Multiplying and dividing fractions

On page 14 we used division to explain fractions: $\frac{3}{5}$ was the number produced from the division 3 ÷ 5. In many textbooks fractions are explained by taking a cake, or pizza, or bar of chocolate (fractions often seem to involve food!) and dividing it into 5 or some other number of equal parts. The parts are then given out to various people. So one person might get $\frac{3}{5}$ while another gets $\frac{2}{5}$. Fractions are explained as fractions *of* something. Although the whole something is often given as a single cake or pizza, this can be very confusing. Fractions are often fractions of several objects ('There were 40 people in the room; three-quarters of them were women') or fractions of something smaller than 1 ('As there are three of you, I'll split this remaining piece of pie into thirds'). It is better not to rely on such diagrams.

In dealing with multiplication and division of fractions you may have wondered about issues like these:

> Why does 'of' mean 'multiply' with fractions?

> Why must fractions be of the same kind to add and subtract, but not to multiply or divide?

> Why is divide 'turn upside-down and multiply' with fractions?

> Can multiplication of fractions be seen as 'repeated addition' as with whole numbers?

Part of the reason many people have problems is because the meaning of fractions changes. Fractions are first of all operators. So, three-sevenths operates on quantities: you can split the quantity into sevenths and then take three of the parts. This can be seen as taking three copies of one-seventh of something. It is then not too difficult a step to consider what happens when you take three-sevenths of three-fifths of something.

The use of words such as 'three-sevenths' is deliberate here. It is to help you think about the meaning of the fractions.

If you look back to the introduction to rational numbers on page 14, you will see that a fraction becomes a label for a point, and then a number. This move to regarding three-sevenths as a number, divorced from any context of calculating three-sevenths of something, is subtle and sophisticated.

Rather than simply repeating methods for multiplying fractions that you have probably met many times before, the following tasks are designed to help you think about the nature of multiplying fractions.

Task 18	Multiplying fractions

Above, you were asked to consider three-sevenths as three copies of one-seventh. The following ask you to express other quantities as 'copies of'.

(a) What are one-half of two-sevenths, and one-third of three-sevenths, in terms of 'copies of'?

(b) By thinking in terms of 'copies of', express the following in terms of parts of a whole:

  (i) one-third of one-fifth of a whole, two-thirds of one-fifth of a whole

  (ii) one-quarter of one-seventh of a whole, two-quarters of one-seventh of a whole

  (iii) one-third of two-fifths of a whole, two-thirds of two-fifths of a whole

(c) Make up more problems as in part (b). Write your questions and answers in fraction notation.

Comment

This activity is posed using words in order to emphasize the operator role of the number-names. It is useful when looking for patterns to use ordinary number-names. Notice that there is a sense of dividing up a whole into parts, and there is a number pattern to do with tops and bottoms which provides an equivalent 'single' operation.

Division of fractions can be thought of in a similar sense. Remember that a statement such as 7 ÷ 2 means 'How many twos are there in seven?'

Task 19	Dividing fractions

Answer the following questions, paying attention to the patterns of numbers in each case. The following questions are indicators of a string of questions which can be used to draw attention to the fact that division of fractions is embedded in the language of fractions and of division.

▶ How many halves are in one? In two? In three? In … ?

▶ How many thirds are in one? In two? In three? In … ?

▶ How many quarters are in … ?

▶ … ?

What is the general pattern? (It should have emerged before you got to this point!)

Answer the next set of questions similarly.

▶ How many one-thirds are in one? How many two-thirds are in two? In three? …

▶ How many two-thirds are in two? In two twos? In two threes? …
In two thumps? In two bananas? In blog? In seven? In eight? In nine? …

▶ How many two-fifths are in two? In two twos? In two threes? …
In two thumps? In two bananas? In blog? In seven? In eight? In nine? …

▶ How many three-fifths are in three? In three twos? In three threes? …
In three thumps? In three bananas? In blog? In seven? In eight? In nine? …

Comment

The intention here is that you start to recognize the pattern in the language and, by being able to say it in 'silly' examples, you can think what the answer must be with other numbers. After becoming fluent in carrying out these tasks, it will help to write them down in fraction notation.

Multiplying decimals

When you have to multiply decimals without a calculator, you probably have some rules that you turn to. Two examples of these rules are:

▶ when multiplying by 10 or 100, move the decimal point one or two places to the right;

▶ when multiplying e.g. 2.42 by 1.8 you work out how many decimal places there are in the answer by adding those in the two numbers.

Many people have such rules which they learned when they were taught how to carry out the calculations. There are various versions of these rules (do you move the decimal point or move the digits, do you line up the decimal points when multiplying or not?) which can lead to uncertainty. This section examines some of these difficulties.

Multiplying and dividing by powers of 10

Consider the multiplication 34.712 × 100 = 3471.2. What is happening with the 'move the decimal point' rule? It is easiest to see by laying out the numbers to show the values of each place:

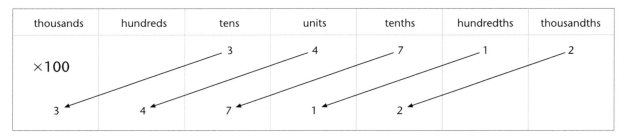

thousands	hundreds	tens	units	tenths	hundredths	thousandths
×100		3	4	7	1	2
3	4	7	1	2		

The decimal point does not actually move anywhere, it is the digits that move. To multiply by 10, the digits move one place to the left; to multiply by 100, the digits move two places to the left, and so on. Similarly, to divide by 10, the digits move one place to the right; to divide by 100, the digits move two places to the right, etc.

This is rather like talking about 'the sun rising in the morning'. It is the Earth that is rotating, rather than the sun moving.

However, most of us imagine the decimal point moving. It is important to remember that imagining the decimal point moving is a quick method rather than an explanation of how, or why, the method works.

The rule for decimal places

Many people try to remember a rule for how many decimal places there will be after multiplying decimals. It is more reliable to work out an estimate of the answer rather than trying to remember a rule.

Consider the calculation 3.6×2.4. An approximation is:

$3.6 \approx 4$ and $2.4 \approx 2$. Because $4 \times 2 = 8$, then $3.6 \times 2.4 \approx 8$.

The actual answer is 8.64 which is approximately equal to 8. The approximation means that you can work out the magnitude of the answer. That is, you can find out if it is going to be about 8 or 80 or 0.8.

Task 20	Estimate and calculate

Use a calculator to find the following:

(a) 12.6×7.9 (b) 100.3×22.67

Comment

Finding an approximation first means that you will know if your answer is of the correct magnitude. When using a calculator, it is very easy to type in the wrong number or for the calculator to give a false result if the batteries are low. You need to know if the answer you are getting is reasonable.

Task 21	Going down

Now try this question:

52.3×0.4

Comment

Some students are surprised at the answer. This is usually because they believe that multiplying always gives a larger answer and dividing a smaller one. With fractions and decimals this is not always the case. Try multiplying other numbers by 0.4. Do they also decrease? Explore with your calculator to find the range of numbers which decrease other numbers when multiplying.

Ratio

Ratio is a method of comparing one thing with another. It is essentially a scaling method ('this is three times as much', 'reduce it by a quarter'), so multiplication and division are the operations involved.

For example, when cooks need to adapt a recipe for more people, they use ratio to scale up the amounts needed.

Recipes Task 22

In a recipe for lamb stew that will feed 6 people you would need 900 g boneless stewing lamb. How would you alter the amounts of the meat if you were trying to feed:

(a) 12 people, or (b) 3 people?

Although this ratio of meat to people can be used, chefs often use a rule of thumb. One is to allow 150 g of meat per person for up to 10 people; for more than 10 people, allow 125 g per person.

Comment

To alter the recipe for 12 people you need to double the amount of meat, whereas for 3 people you halve the amounts. This is relatively easy to do, but to alter the amounts to feed 11 people would be more tricky. In reality you would probably make enough for 12 people and have a bit left over.

The last task involved only one ingredient. Ratio is also used in getting the correct balance between ingredients. For example, when making a sponge cake you need 4 oz flour, to 4 oz butter, to 4 oz sugar, and 2 eggs. To make a sponge cake you need the same amount of flour, butter and sugar with half the number of eggs. So if you wanted to make a cake with 6 oz of flour you would need 6 oz flour, to 6 oz butter, to 6 oz sugar, and 3 eggs. Cooks are really comparing the amount of flour, to butter, to sugar, and eggs. There is a problem with this way of describing the mixture. In mathematical terms, each of the ingredients should be in the same measures. This means that you cannot have ounces and numbers of eggs in the same ratio (and of course, it wouldn't work in metric measures!).

Cooks often refer to this as a 4, 4, 4, 2 mixture.

Another everyday use of ratios is in the garden. For example, the instructions on a plant food box include the following.

For general garden feeding you need:

2 teaspoons of plant food dissolved in 5 litres of water.

For house plants you need:

1 teaspoon of plant food dissolved in 10 litres of water.

Solutions Task 23

Are these two solutions the same strength? If not, then which is stronger?

Comment

If you wanted to make 10 litres of the solution for general garden feeding then you would need:

4 teaspoons of plant food dissolved in 10 litres of water.

This means there are four times as many teaspoons of food in this mixture than in the one for house plants. This is therefore a stronger mixture.

Would you use the same method for solving the following question?

Task 24	Travelling

In 15 minutes I travelled 18 km. How far would I go in 25 minutes if I travelled at the same speed?

Comment

If in 15 min, I travel 18 km, then in 5 min I travel 18 km ÷ 3 = 6 km.
So in 25 min, I would travel 6 km × 5 = 30 km.

This method is a typical mental method.

Another possible solution is below. It is called the **unitary method**.

In 15 min I travel 18 km.
So in 1 min I travel $\frac{18}{15}$ or 1.2 km.
Therefore in 25 min I will travel 25 × 1.2 km = 30 km.

This is called the unitary method because you find the value for 1 (or unity) before finding any multiple of that amount.

Calculating with percentages

Recall the section on page 22 about percentage notation.

Percentages can be calculated using either fractions or decimals, although with a calculator, decimals are usually easier. You can also use the $\boxed{\%}$ key on your calculator. How the $\boxed{\%}$ key works depends on the calculator type; you will need to consult your manual if you choose to use it.

Finding a percentage of something is straightforward.

Task 25	Percentage

A building society offers 95% mortgages to first-time buyers. How much would the Smiths get on a house valued at £35 750?

Comment

95% = 0.95

So 95% of £35 750 = 0.95 × £35 750
= £33 962.50

Two issues often cause difficulty with percentages:

▶ finding percentage increases or decreases;

▶ finding successive percentages, for example calculating VAT and a service change on a bill – does the order of calculating matter?

You have already seen a method of calculating VAT mentally (see pages 25–26).

Many people work out a problem such as:

Find what £322 is after a 15% increase

by carrying out a two-stage calculation, first finding 15% and then adding it on. This method works, of course, but you can use your awareness of the connections between percentages and decimals to simplify the calculation. Finding a percentage increase of 15% is the same as finding 115% of the original. This percentage can be written as a decimal, 1.15, and then calculated in the same way as any other percentage. So:

£322 increased by 15% = 1.15 × 322 = £370.30

The same applies to decreases: a 10% discount will give 90% of the original, so multiply by 0.9.

You should check that this gives the same result as the two-stage method.

VAT	Task 26

On many bills, for example in restaurants, VAT is added at $17\frac{1}{2}$% and sometimes also a service charge of 15%. Does it make any difference to what you have to pay if the VAT is added first then the service charge, or vice versa?

Make up some examples to try. Remember to keep them simple. The examples are special cases; from these examples you are trying to work out what will always happen – the general case.

Comment

Take a restaurant bill of £16.

Adding VAT first means calculating $(100\% + 17\frac{1}{2}\%)$ of £16:

$117\frac{1}{2}$% of £16 = 1.175 × £16 = £18.80

Adding the service charge on top is (100% + 15%) of £18.80:

115% of £18.80 = 1.15 × £18.80 = £21.62

Adding the extras the other way round:

115% of £16 = 1.15 × £16 = £18.40
$117\frac{1}{2}$% of £18.40 = £21.62

This is the same total amount. Can you see why this is so?

Looking at the general case can sometimes make a result clearer. Suppose the amount of the bill is, say, £n.

Adding the VAT first gives:

$117\frac{1}{2}$% of £n = 1.175 × £n

Adding the service charge now gives:

115% of (1.175 × £n) = 1.15 × 1.175 × £n

At this point you may be able to see that the order does not matter. Multiplying by the two decimals 1.15 and 1.175 can take place in any order.

This is an example of the commutative property of multiplication. See *Number and algebra*, page 80.

If you need convincing further, the extras can be added the other way round:

$$115\% \text{ of } £n = 1.15 \times £n$$
$$117\tfrac{1}{2}\% \text{ of } (1.15 \times £n) = 1.175 \times 1.15 \times £n$$

Since $1.15 \times 1.175 \times £n = 1.175 \times 1.15 \times £n$ the answer will always be the same.

Measures

The importance of standard measurements becomes evident when you want to communicate a measurement to another person. You could go into a DIY store with a piece of string to measure the length of the window blind that you need. But if you needed to order a blind then including the piece of string with the order form would not be acceptable – a standard measure would be needed.

Units of measurement

In the UK there are three systems of units of measurement in use: imperial, metric and SI (Système Internationale). When imperial measures were first used they were based on the sort of amounts that people commonly used, or on parts of the human body. This means that the relationships between units are unplanned and seem very arbitrary. By contrast, the metric system was designed as a whole with the relationships between units following a logical pattern. SI units are a version of metric units constructed to make international communication easier, especially in science and engineering.

Each system is considered separately and then connections between them are examined.

The metric system

Metric measures were designed to fit together by being based on multiples of ten. For example, the distance cycled in a day is likely to be given in kilometres (abbreviated to km), a person's height in metres (m) and their waist measurement in centimetres (cm). The prefixes 'kilo' and 'centi', together with 'milli', are used throughout the metric system. Here they are illustrated with measures of length:

'kilo' means 1000, so a kilometre (km) is 1000 metres;

'centi' means $\frac{1}{100}$, so a centimetre (cm) is $\frac{1}{100}$ metre or 0.01 m (there are 100 centimetres in a metre);

'milli' means $\frac{1}{1000}$, so a millimetre (mm) is $\frac{1}{1000}$ metre or 0.001 m (there are 1000 millimetres in a metre).

There are other prefixes, much less commonly used – 'deci', 'deca', 'hecto':

1 decametre = 10 metres ('deca' means 10);

1 hectometre = 100 metres ('hecto' means 100);

1 decimetre = $\frac{1}{10}$ metre or 0.1 m ('deci' means $\frac{1}{10}$).

It is easy to confuse the words 'decimetre' and 'decametre' (which is possibly the reason they are seldom used).

Of course these metric prefixes ('kilo' etc.) are used for other units besides those of length: kilograms (kg), millilitres (ml) and so on. These simple relationships mean that it is easy to convert measurements in, say, centimetres to millimetres or metres; for example, 2170 mm = 217 cm = 2.17 m.

Imperial (British) system

By contrast with the metric system, the numerical relationships between the imperial units, whether of length, capacity, weight (mass) have no logical basis:

12 inches = 1 foot
3 feet = 1 yard
1760 yards = 1 mile

16 ounces = 1 pound
14 pounds = 1 stone
2240 pounds = 1 ton

The introduction of metrication means that imperial units are gradually going out of use in the UK though miles, yards, feet and inches will continue to be used for road traffic signs and related measurements of speed and distance.

Converting between units is thus quite complicated. For example:

2170 inches = 180 feet 10 inches = 60 yards 10 inches

Notice also that decimals are rarely used with imperial measures (2170 inches would be 180.833 33… feet).

Système Internationale (SI) system

The SI system is a version of the metric system used in science and engineering. Its aim was to simplify and standardize the prefixes ('kilo' etc.) and so to avoid mistakes due to misplaced decimal points. For example, the base unit of length in the SI system is the metre and all other units are related to it in multiples of 1000. There are 1000 metres in 1 kilometre (km) and 1 millimetre (mm) is one thousandth of a metre. The prefixes used in the SI system are standard for any quantity within it so if you know the base units you can work out the naming and the values of the rest. Here are some of the prefixes used:

Sometimes thousands are separated by commas e.g. 10,000; however, using a space prevents confusion with the continental system of using a comma to separate whole and decimal parts (the UK uses the decimal point).

Prefix	Symbol	Figures	Words	Powers of 10
giga	G	1 000 000 000	a thousand millions (a billion)	10^9
mega	M	1 000 000	a million	10^6
kilo	k	1 000	a thousand	10^3
		1	one	10^0
milli	m	0.001	a thousandth	10^{-3}
micro	μ	0.000 001	a millionth	10^{-6}
nano	n	0.000 000 001	a thousand millionth	10^{-9}

μ, the symbol used for 'micro', is the Greek letter pronounced 'mu'.

You may not need to calculate with some of the very large or very small numbers in the table, but in the world of computing, for example, 'mega' and 'giga' are often used (though not very precisely!).

Notice that centimetres, for example, are not used in the SI system, because a centimetre is $\frac{1}{100}$ metre and $\frac{1}{100}$ ths of a unit are not used. If you look in furniture or kitchen catalogues you might notice that some give the measurements in centimetres and others in millimetres.

Task 27	Appropriate units

Strong views are often expressed about the use of millimetres as opposed to centimetres and vice versa. Some engineers maintain that 'centimetres don't exist'! Write down points for and against the use of millimetres as opposed to centimetres.

Comment

You may have included some of the following points made during a discussion between two teachers from the same secondary school:

> The kids arrive in Year 7 and they don't know what a millimetre is and of course everybody in D&T and everybody in engineering all use millimetres. It is the basic unit and the first thing you do is bang your head up against the wall because you say 'right we are going to do a 10 mm border' and the first child would say 'I don't know what that is – I haven't got millimetres on my ruler'. (D&T teacher)

> But you can't visualize a millimetre – it's a little tiny thing ... but I can understand why you are working in millimetres because then you are not messing about with a decimal point. (Mathematics teacher)

> Open University/Design Council (1997) *Maths by Design*

Numbers and measurement

When a measure is expressed in different units the relationships between numbers is exact: 2170 mm is identical to 217 cm. However, actual measurement using instruments is always approximate: it is not possible to say that the width of a room measures *exactly* 2170 mm. This is partly due to human error in, for example, lining up the measuring mark exactly opposite the object being measured; but also because of the nature of measuring. Even when you had measured as carefully as you could, if you were able to magnify around the measuring mark, there would still be a further variation from your mark. With digital electronic measuring devices this is evident. When an electronic weighing scale that is able to measure to the nearest milligram produces a reading of 34 mg, then the object it measured might be slightly above or slightly below 34 mg. The scale would be unable to distinguish between those weights.

Showing the accuracy of a measurement

In everyday tasks such as cooking or DIY the small errors that creep into measuring are more than offset by the skill (or not!) of the person doing it. In work situations such as a hospital pharmacy or in manufacturing, knowing the size of measurement errors is crucial so they need to be both quantified and stated. There are several ways of doing this. As an example take a measurement such as 5 g of a substance weighed on digital scales which read to the nearest 1 g. This means that the mass could be as low as 4.5 g which is called the lower bound (or limit) or it could be almost (but not quite) 5.5 g at the upper bound (or limit).

The usual practice for rounding a value is that if it ends in 5 (e.g. 35 or 7.5) it rounds up. So here 4.5 would round up to 5, but 5.5 would round up to 6.

This range of possible values can be expressed in several different ways:

> 5 g to the nearest 1 g
> 5 ± 0.5 g
> a value m, where $4.5 \leq m < 5.5$

or in a picture:

When the accuracy is expressed in the form $\pm e$, e is called the **error bound**.

4.5   5   5.5

(The filled-in circle shows that the lowest value is included; the open circle shows that 5.5 is not included.)

Using the convention $m \pm e$ quoted above, express the range of possible values for:

(a) 25 minutes measured to the nearest minute;

(b) 400 ml measured to the nearest 5 ml;

(c) 180 °C measured to the nearest 10 °C;

(d) 20 cm measured to the nearest 0.2 cm.

Comment

(a) $25 \pm \frac{1}{2}$ minute

(b) 400 ± 2.5 ml

(c) 180 ± 5 °C

(d) 20 ± 0.1 cm

This way of stating errors uses the actual value of the error and is called the **absolute error**. Sometimes errors are given as a percentage of the value and are then called **relative errors**. For example, suppose sugar is weighed on scales which read to the nearest 5 grams. With this particular set of scales every reading will have the same absolute error, that is ± 2.5 grams. But this amount of error will have a far greater effect on a small reading than on a large one. To express this relative error we can use percentages.

For an item weighing 25 grams:

$$\frac{2.5}{25} \times 100 = 10\%$$

so the relative error is 25 grams ± 10%.

For an item weighing 250 grams:

$$\frac{2.5}{250} \times 100 = 1\%$$

so the relative error is 250 grams ± 1%.

Using measurements in calculations

It is important to appreciate that any errors made in measuring will be affected during any subsequent calculation. For example, if the length of an item is measured and the reading is recorded as 645 mm, this implies an accuracy of 645 mm to the nearest millimetre so the error could be ± 0.5 mm. If you multiply this by 10, the error becomes:

$$\pm\, 0.5 \times 10 = 5 \text{ mm}$$

It is recognized that measurements of manufactured items cannot be completely accurate so the amount of error is called tolerance, an allowable variation. Tolerances of resistors used in electronics are quoted in percentages so a resistor with a tolerance of 5% is of better quality than one with a tolerance of 10%.

Other measures

Aspects of area, volume and angle are discussed in *Geometry and algebra*.

Some other things you might measure are area, volume, capacity, time, temperature, mass and angles.

Area

Area is the amount of space within a plane (2D) shape. In the metric system area is measured in square metres (m^2) or square centimetres (cm^2).

Volume and capacity

Volume is the amount of space inside a 3D shape. Solid shapes have a volume measured in cubic metres (m^3) or cubic centimetres (cm^3). More commonly, litres (l) or millilitres (ml) are used (a litre is 1000 cm^3).

Angle

Angle is an amount of turn and is often measured in everyday life in terms of complete turns or right angles. For more accurate measurement a protractor or a circular angle measurer is used and the units are degrees (symbol °). The instruction 'turn right' implies turning to the right through a right angle or 90°. Turning half right would be about half this angle, i.e. 45°. If you use a scientific calculator you may be familiar with radians:

π is the ratio of the circumference to the diameter for any circle.

$$1 \text{ complete turn} = 360° = 2\pi \text{ radians}$$

Time

Common units of time are seconds, minutes, hours and days.

60 seconds = 1 minute
60 minutes = 1 hour
24 hours = 1 day
7 days = 1 week

The SI base unit for time is the second. Small amounts of time will be measured in milliseconds (ms) or even microseconds (μs).

Temperature

The common unit of temperature is degrees Celsius (°C). The SI unit of temperature is the kelvin (K) but this unit is mainly used in science. Many people still use the Fahrenheit system (°F), especially for hot weather ('It was in the nineties') and body temperature ('Her temperature was up to 103').

Mass

The terms 'mass' and 'weight' can cause confusion. **Mass** is the amount of matter in an object and does not alter wherever you are in the universe. The SI unit of mass is the gram. **Weight** depends on the force of gravity on the object and is measured in newtons. For most purposes, the mass and weight of an object are treated as the same because the gravitational force does not vary much on Earth. If an object was moved to the Moon, although its mass would remain the same, its weight would decrease because gravity on the Moon is less than on Earth.

Metric units of mass are always used in science, and grams and kilograms are becoming the usual units of mass in supermarkets.

Conversion from one system of units to another

Even with a single system of units it can be confusing to convert one unit to another, especially in units such as those for area.

Square units	Task 29

The area of a shape is 1.5 m^2. What is this in cm^2? (It might help to draw a quick sketch.)

Comment

It is tempting to say that because there are 100 centimetres in 1 metre:

$$1.5 \text{ m}^2 = 1.5 \times 100 = 150 \text{ cm}^2$$

This is not the correct answer. If you need convincing, draw a square and mark the sides 1 m = 100 cm. The area of the square is:

$$1 \text{ m} \times 1 \text{ m} = 1 \text{ m}^2 \quad \text{or} \quad 100 \text{ cm} \times 100 \text{ cm} = 10\ 000 \text{ cm}^2$$

So an area of 1.5 m^2 equals $1.5 \times 10\ 000 = 15\ 000$ cm^2.

Many people refer to a 1 kg bag of sugar as 'a 2-pound bag' or say 'half-a-pound of butter' when they refer to a 250 g packet.

Because both metric and imperial units are used in the UK, people frequently have problems when measures are expressed in a system different to the one they normally use. Most people find that they are confident with only one system of units for any particular purpose. This may be metric for some measures and imperial for others. They may, for example, feel happy measuring furniture in centimetres or buying petrol in litres, but read their car speed in miles per hour and buy their vegetables in pounds and ounces. Where there is a need in everyday use to convert from one system to another, most people use easy reference points such as:

> 30 cm is about the same length as 1 foot;
> 1 metre is slightly bigger than a yard;
> 5 miles is about the same as 8 kilometres.

These are usually good enough.

This is another example of ratio as a scaling.

For more exact conversions you need to use a calculation method using a **conversion (or scale) factor**. If you have several conversions to make, it may be quicker to use the constant facility on your calculator. If you wanted to refer to the results later you could produce a **conversion graph** or a **conversion table**. All these methods require an equivalence point from one system to the other. They are all discussed below.

You may find that, like many people, you get confused about which way round you have to do a conversion calculation using a scale factor. For example, if you are told that:

> 4.55 litres = 1 gallon

Gallons and litres are used as conversion examples for the rest of this section.

what scale factor do you multiply 6 gallons by to change into litres? And to change 35 litres into gallons? A diagram can help:

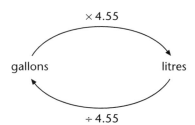

A US gallon is smaller than a UK one (it is 3.79 litres).

Converting one way is 'doing', in this case multiplying by 4.55. Converting the other way is 'undoing'; here, dividing by 4.55.

For both methods you need to know that 1 UK gallon = 4.55 litres.

Converting

Convert:

(a) 6 gallons to litres; (b) 35 litres to gallons.

Comment

(a) involves converting from gallons to litres. To do this you multiply the number of gallons by 4.55. So:

6 gallons = 6 × 4.55 litres = 27.30 litres

(b) involves converting from litres to gallons. This is reversing the process and so undoing the previous type of calculation. Hence, 35 is divided by 4.55:

35 litres = 35 ÷ 4.55 gallons = 7.69 gallons (rounded to 2 decimal places)

Gallons	Litres
0	0
1	4.55
2	9.10
3	13.65
4	18.20
5	22.75
6	27.30
7	31.85
8	36.40
9	40.95
10	45.50

Calculator constant and conversion table

If you have to carry out a series of conversion calculations of the same kind, a good method is to use the constant facility on your calculator. This could be used to draw up a conversion table. You will see such tables for litres and gallons on petrol pumps; one converting gallons to litres is given in the margin. A disadvantage of the table is that conversions from whole numbers of litres to gallons are not easy.

Converting back

Create a table for converting litres to gallons (remember, you need to *divide* by 4.55) using the constant facility on your calculator. A suitable range would be every 5 litres from 0 to 50. (Do this in a similar way to that explained for converting marks out of 65 to percentages as shown on page 30.)

Graphical method

Setting up a conversion graph takes time but once it is done the graph provides a quick visual method for converting units in both directions. It involves mapping one set of measurements onto another. The drawback is that the accuracy is limited by the scale used.

Drawing a conversion graph

Once again work with a range of 0 to 10 gallons. The technique for all conversion graphs that involve a constant scale factor (4.55 in this case) is to produce a straight line joining two known conversion values.

Two known values here are:

0 gallons = 0 litres
1 gallon = 4.55 litres

These would be close together on the graph, so for more accuracy a better second pair of values would be:

10 gallons = 45.5 litres

On a piece of graph paper, draw in two axes as in the diagram and label the horizontal axis (or *x*-axis) 'gallons' and the vertical axis (or *y*-axis) 'litres'. Mark in an equally spaced scale for gallons (0–10) and one for litres (0–50).

Plot the two points (0, 0) and (10, 45.5) and join up the points to make a straight line.

Comment

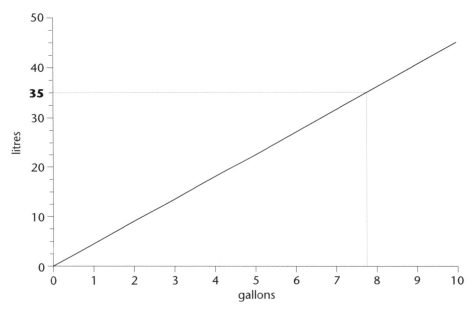

Task 33   **Using the graph**

Suppose you bought 35 litres of petrol at the garage and wanted to know how many gallons that is. Use the graph to find out.

Comment

Drawing a horizontal line from the 35 mark to meet the graph line and then drawing a line down to meet the *x*-axis (as in the diagram), you can see that 35 litres is about 7.7 gallons.

This does not give as accurate an answer as the calculation method.

When using the information from both methods you can see that:

number of litres = 4.55 × number of gallons

If we call the number of litres y and the equivalent number of gallons x then

$y = 4.55x$

All graphs involving a constant scale factor are of this form, $y = kx$, where k is a fixed number. In the case of changing gallons to litres, $k = 4.55$.

If you have access to a graphics calculator, you can produce both a graph that gives x and y values, and a conversion table.

Graphs of this kind are discussed in *Number and algebra*, page 92.

Task 34   *Using a graphics calculator*

Put in the function $y = 4.55x$, set the WINDOW to the same setting as in the graphing task above and draw the graph. This should be a straight line passing through the origin (0, 0). Use the TRACE key to move the cursor along the line. The coordinates of the cursor will be displayed. In this case the x values are the number of gallons and the y values are the equivalent number of litres. If your calculator has a TABLE function set the table to start at 0 and go up in steps of 0.5. The TABLE can now be used to show equivalent amounts for gallons and litres.

Comment

If you can use a spreadsheet on a computer, you can produce tables and graphs in a similar fashion.

Links between quantities: rates and compound units

Compound units

The units discussed so far have been for single quantities, but some quantities expressed as rates (for example, speeds) require **compound units**.

Speeds of vehicles such as cars, bicycles or trains are usually given as miles per hour or kilometres per hour. A sprinter's speed may be quoted in metres per second; a child's growth in centimetres per year. Each of these units are given as:

unit of distance *per* unit of time

Other examples of rates are:

density, measured in grams per cubic centimetre;
rate of flow, measured in litres per minute;
fuel consumption, measured in miles per gallon.

Rates can usually be recognized by the use of the word 'per'.

It is usual in imperial units to abbreviate miles per hour as mph, or miles per gallon as mpg. In the metric and SI systems 'p' is not used as an abbreviation for 'per'. Instead, metres per second is written m/s or m s^{-1}.

$1 \text{ km}^2 \xrightarrow{\times 807} 807 \text{ people}$

With rates you have to interpret the numbers with more care than when using simple units. One of the difficulties of rates is that they can be read in two ways. For example, the population density of a region might be 807 people/km^2. This means that there are on average 807 people for each square kilometre.

$1 \div 807 \xleftarrow{\div 807} 1 \text{ person}$
$= 0.00124 \text{ km}^2$

But this figure might be given the other way round. How much space does each person have? In this case the figure would be found by reversing (undoing) the scaling.

That is, one person has:

$$1 \div 807 = 0.001\ 24 \text{ km}^2$$

This small value is not easy to interpret, so it might be preferable in m^2. This converts as:

$$1000 \times 1000 \times 0.001\ 24 \text{ m}^2 = 1240 \text{ m}^2$$

which is the amount of space per person.

Task 35	Comparing fuel consumptions

Consider the situation when a new model of a car is brought out. If the fuel consumption of the new model is 30 mpg as against 25 mpg, what does this tell you?

Comment

You will probably say that 30 mpg is better than 25 mpg as the car travels more miles for the same amount of petrol (one gallon). It is also possible to think about this the other way round. For a journey of 25 miles, the previous model of car used 1 gallon; the new one will not use as much (since it can go 30 miles for 1 gallon). Thus for a fixed length of journey you will use less petrol.

However, if you look at a current brochure for a new car you may be surprised by some of the figures given for fuel consumption. For example an extract from a VW brochure (1997) gives the fuel consumption of a 1.0L model Polo as:

	mpg	litres per 100 km
Urban driving	36.2	7.8
Non-urban driving	56.5	5.0

As you might expect, the imperial values show that fuel consumption is better (in terms of getting more miles for each gallon of petrol for out-of-town driving). But how do you interpret the metric values? Instead of apparently increasing from urban driving to non-urban driving, they go down. Yet in each case the figures quoted are for the same model of the same car. In the second case, you may have noticed that the rate of consumption is the other way round, as the number of litres for each 100 kilometres of distance travelled. It gives how much fuel is used for a fixed distance.

Rates can be complicated to understand and interpret. As they are mainly used for comparison purposes (in the above case in order to make decisions about efficiency or value for money) it is important to know what the figures are telling you.

Check whether the figures for the Polo car given above are correct. Do you agree that 36.2 mpg is equivalent to 7.8 litre per 100 km?

There are three conversions to carry out:

This task is quite exacting. If you can carry it out successfully, you have a good grasp of conversions.

⬗ miles to kilometres;

⬗ gallons to litres;

⬗ *either* miles per gallon to gallons per mile
or kilometres per litre to litres per 100 kilometres.

You will need two conversion factors:

1 gallon = 4.55 litres
1 mile = 1.609 km

Comment

Here is one possible solution. You may have reached the same answer but have done it in a different way or in a different order. That does not matter. The important thing is that you can follow your working and someone else seeing it for the first time could also follow it.

The rate of petrol consumption is given as 36.2 mpg miles per gallon.

Changing gallons to litres. Since 4.55 litres is approximately equal to 1 gallon I will get fewer miles for one litre:

If you have access to a graphics calculator you can see the stages on the screen. Set your calculator to read 3 decimal places.

$36.2 \div 4.55 = 7.956$ miles per litre

Changing miles to kilometres. 1 mile = 1.609 km approximately

$7.956 \times 1.609 = 12.801$ km per litre

But the table shows litres per kilometre and not vice versa. Taking the reciprocal:

If you wondered why 3 decimal places was suggested earlier it is this stage that makes the difference.

12.801 km per litre $= \dfrac{1}{12.801}$ litre per km $= 0.078$ litre per km

To find how many litres for 100 km, multiply the answer by 100:

$0.078 \times 100 = 7.8$ litre per 100 km (rounded to 1 decimal place)

This is the value give*n in the table.*

In task 36 you have used imperial and metric units, compound units, conversion factors, rates of change and their interpretation, multiplication, division, taking a reciprocal, rounding.

A useful way of reviewing a topic like measures is to make a diagram showing different measures and their connections. Look back over this section on measures and make a map or plan showing the main issues and show how they connect or lead on from another.

Comment

An example of the start of such a map showing common quantities and units is shown below.

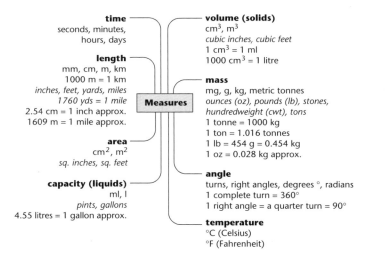

Here is another map trying to build up links with compound measures:

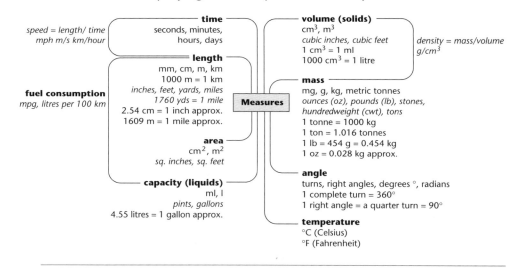

Further reading

Doug French (1992) *Mental Methods in Mathematics*, Mathematical Association.

SCAA (1997) *The Teaching and Assessment of Number at Key Stages 1–3*, SCAA Discussion Paper no. 10, QCA.

If you have access to the internet you will find further details about units and measures in the article 'Dictionary of units and measurement' at:

http://www.ex.ac.uk/cimt/dictunit/dictunit.htm

3. Statistics and measuring

Introduction

For too many students at all levels, statistics is their least popular subject. Traditionally, statistics courses have involved students learning to use a variety of calculations and graphs with no idea of why. This can be pointless and demoralizing. Statistical ideas are more effectively and enjoyably learnt when they are seen to be helpful in solving a problem or answering a question, rather than simply as things to do and skills to learn. For example, it is one thing to learn how to calculate a mean or draw a histogram, but it is quite another to be able to use them sensibly in context. Knowing when to use statistical skills is best learnt by applying them in real or plausible situations where the outcomes have some meaning and significance. Where possible, the statistical ideas in this chapter have been presented as they might crop up in the context of a statistical investigation, which is characterized by the following key stages, the PCAI stages:

Stage P   Pose a question.
Stage C   Collect relevant data.
Stage A   Analyse the data.
Stage I   Interpret the results.

The various statistical techniques that you will need to know tend to crop up at recognizable stages. For example, choosing samples and designing questionnaires may be required at stage C, 'Collect relevant data'. Stage A, 'Analyse the data', is likely to involve calculations, tables and graphs. This is where calculators and computers can be of considerable help. Although their use is not essential to the study of this chapter, it would be of benefit if you could have access to a suitable item of technology to help with the data-crunching. Of particular use in statistical work is a graphics (large screen) calculator and a spreadsheet or database on a computer. The technological skills of using them will not be taught here, but some screen pictures are included to indicate where and how they might be used.

In order to save time and space, you will not be asked to pose questions for investigation yourself. Because stage P cannot be used, some of the data you will need in this chapter will be supplied for you. Clearly, to some extent this contradicts the spirit of engaging in a purposeful statistical investigation as described above. However, the main job of this chapter is to set out the summarizing and graphing techniques that would normally crop up at stage A of an investigation. First, though, there is a short section on collecting data.

Collecting the data

Designing the questionnaire

You will commonly see the word 'data' used either as a plural noun ('The data are gathered by questionnaire') or as a singular noun ('My data is stored on the computer'). In statistics 'data' is often used as a plural.

Data can derive from various sources – direct measurement (perhaps from an experiment), responses from a survey or data gleaned from other sources like books and newspapers. Where data are gathered from a survey, this may involve designing and administering a questionnaire. Questionnaire design is a large topic in its own right which cannot be explored at length here. However, here are a few simple guidelines for good questionnaire design.

Avoid asking questions that:

- you don't really need to know the answer to (this uses up valuable good will);
- can't be answered (for example, 'How healthy are you?');
- may provide you with ambiguous responses that can't easily be processed (for example, 'Where do your parents live?');
- are likely to cause offence (for example, questions that are an unnecessary invasion of privacy);
- are biased (for example, 'Do you agree that murderous thugs should receive stiffer prison sentences?');
- include overlapping or missing categories in the options provided (for example 'age categories: 0–20, 20–40, 40–60, etc.').

Choosing the sample

Like questionnaire design, sampling comprises many more issues than there is space to explore here. The need for sampling arises because we may wish to get information from a large number of people but not be able or willing to contact them all. Many decisions in life are made on the basis of sampling. For example, you may want to check that your soup is exactly to your liking. Rather than drink it all, you taste a spoonful – a sample. To ensure that it is representative of the whole pot, you may give the soup a vigorous stir beforehand. Sampling in statistics is guided by the need to ensure that the sample is as representative as possible of the population from which it is taken. For example, sampling day-time shoppers may under-represent office workers, sampling just the people in a bus queue may under-represent car drivers, and so on.

Categories and measures

Data collection usually involves putting into categories (names) or measuring on a scale. Think of the data taken by the police from a suspect. Some of the information they might wish to record is:

Name, Address, Gender, Age, Height, Hair colour, Eye colour, Shoe size.

Collecting these items of data sometimes involves putting in a category, and sometimes requires measuring. The next task will get you thinking about the difference between these two ways of recording information.

Consider the following three out of the eight variables listed above:

Eye colour, Height, Shoe size.

Try to decide whether collecting these data involves using categories or measuring on a scale of measure.

Comment

Eye colour – and Name, Address, Gender and Hair colour – are **categories**. On the other hand, Height (and also Age) is something you would **measure** on a scale. Shoe size seems to fall between the two approaches. On the one hand it involves numbers, so might be listed under measuring. But on the other hand, there is only a restricted number of shoe sizes available (you can only have whole and half sizes – you can't have shoe size 7.1927, for example). So, in a sense, shoe sizes can be thought of as categories.

The most useful way of thinking about the various types of variables is to distinguish them as follows:

▶ Where measurement is carried out on a continuous scale of measure the variable is called **continuous**.

▶ Where categories are used (even where these are numbers, as with shoe size) the variable is called **discrete**.

These ways of classifying data are summarized below.

▶ discrete data
  – names
  – discrete numbers

▶ continuous data
  – numbers on a continuous scale of measure

Look once more at the eight variables:

Name, Address, Gender, Age, Height, Hair colour, Eye colour, Shoe size.

(a) Which are numerical and which are names?

(b) Which are discrete numbers and which continuous?

Comment

Age, Height and Shoe size are numerical, while the rest are names.

Shoe size is a discrete number variable, and Age and Height are continuous.

Note that although Age, like most measures of time, is a continuous variable, on a questionnaire most people will state their age rounded down to the full year below (someone who is 30 years and 7 months will say that they are thirty years old), so age data may actually be recorded as discrete numbers.

Young children sometimes describe themselves as 'aged $7\frac{3}{4}$'.

Analysing the data

In this section you will be taken through a simple investigation about name lengths. You will be shown how to handle various calculations and graphs, and will be expected to work through these tasks yourself, based on your own data set.

In a technology lesson, a group of students were constructing jigsaws from the letters of their first names. One student commented that it was tougher on the girls because their names were longer than those of the boys. Not everyone agreed with this view and it soon became the subject of a heated debate and subsequently a statistical investigation in a mathematics lesson. They posed the question: 'Are girls' first names longer or shorter than boys'?'

Task 3	Your data: friends you can count on

Based on people whom you know personally, write down twelve male and twelve female names. Count the number of letters of each name to produce two lists of numbers.

Is this a sensible way of sampling the names?

A similar calculation has been carried out in the table below using fifteen female and fifteen male names selected randomly from a daily newspaper.

Using a spreadsheet, the function 'LEN' can be used to count the word lengths directly.

Name lengths taken from a daily newspaper

Female	Length (F)	Male	Length (M)
Carol	5	Melville	8
Caroline	8	Peter	5
Faye	4	Richard	7
Marina	6	Michael	7
Sophie	6	Brian	5
Caterina	8	Martin	6
Hazel	5	Jack	4
Eileen	6	Hans	4
Jane	4	Jeremy	6
Stella	6	Warren	6
Clare	5	Trevor	6
Teresa	6	Christopher	11
Celia	5	Bill	4
Charlotte	9	Kenny	5
Margaret	8	John	4

It is difficult to compare two lists of numbers (the raw data) sensibly. Looking at the raw data alone, you can't easily get a clear sense of overall patterns and differences. It is difficult even to see how many people there are with each name length. As a first step to making the data easier to handle, it is a good idea to sort the data into order by name length.

These data were sorted (in less than a second!) on a spreadsheet.

On the spreadsheet, the columns were selected two at a time for sorting, to ensure that the correspondence between each person's name and their name length is maintained.

Name data sorted in ascending order

Female	Length (F)	Male	Length (M)
Faye	4	Jack	4
Jane	4	Hans	4
Carol	5	Bill	4
Hazel	5	John	4
Clare	5	Peter	5
Celia	5	Brian	5
Marina	6	Kenny	5
Sophie	6	Martin	6
Eileen	6	Jeremy	6
Stella	6	Warren	6
Teresa	6	Trevor	6
Caroline	8	Richard	7
Caterina	8	Michael	7
Margaret	8	Melville	8
Charlotte	9	Christopher	11

It is now much easier to count the number of people with each name length.

To get a clearer sense of the data it is often useful to use the strategy of visualizing. With statistics this usually involves drawing graphs and diagrams.

Graphing the data

Knowing which graph or diagram to draw is not always obvious – the choice depends partly on the nature of the data and also on the sort of analysis you want to make.

Here are the more common graphs in use:

pie chart, bar chart, pictograph, histogram, boxplot, line graph, scatterplot.

These days, graphs can be drawn easily using a machine – a computer spreadsheet or graphics calculator, for example. Letting the machine do the mechanical part enables you, the user, to put your energies where they are most usefully directed: in thinking about which type of graph would be most helpful in meeting your needs, and in interpreting the graph once it has been drawn.

The question of how to draw these graphs by hand is not covered here. You can gain this information from most basic statistics textbooks – for example, see *Further reading*, Graham and Green (1994) and Graham (1994).

Not all of the graph types given above can be used to represent these name length data (for example, the last two, line graph and scatterplot, would be inappropriate). You will find out later why this is the case. For now, look at the four sets of graphs below, the pie chart, bar chart, pictograph and histogram. Although it is technically possible to use all of these to depict these name length data, some are more appropriate than others. Try to decide how helpful they are in the context of this investigation and begin to think about when their use is sensible and what sort of conclusions can be drawn from them. These issues will be taken up again in the next section, 'Interpreting the results'.

Pie charts

These are pie charts of the name length data:

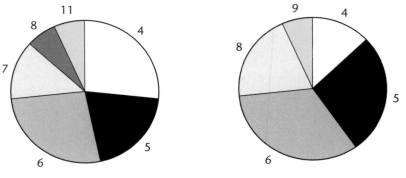

Male name lengths   Female name lengths

With a pie chart, the size of each sector is a measure of its frequency. In the pie chart for female name lengths the sector marked 6 is the largest, reflecting the fact that 6 is the most common female name length. For the pie chart of male name lengths, the sectors 4 and 6 are equal largest.

Bar charts

These are bar charts of the name length data:

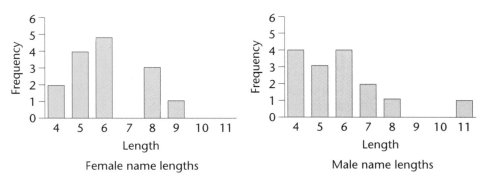

Female name lengths   Male name lengths

With these bar charts, name lengths are shown on the horizontal axis and the frequencies on the vertical axis. Thus, the tallest bar corresponds to that name length which occurred most frequently. The bars on a bar chart can be drawn either vertically (as is the case here) or horizontally. Gaps are drawn between the bars because the data are discrete.

Pictographs

This is a pictograph of the name length data:

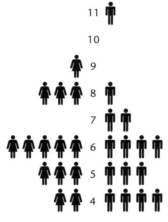

Female name lengths Male name lengths

Pictographs (sometimes called pictograms or ideographs) are similar in construction to bar charts except that the frequency of each category is represented by a line of helpful pictures rather than a bar. As with bar charts, the pictures on a pictograph can be drawn either vertically or horizontally.

Histograms

Like a bar chart, a histogram is a form of block graph. The distinction between a histogram and a bar chart is to do with the sort of data they represent. Whereas a bar chart is used to represent discrete data (i.e. categories or discrete numbers), a histogram represents continuous data (for example, people's heights, weights, ages and so on). This distinction shows up visually according to whether or not there are gaps between adjacent bars: a bar chart should have these gaps (to emphasize the discrete nature of the data) whereas a histogram should be drawn so that adjacent bars touch (to emphasize the continuous nature of the data).

As the name length data is discrete (name lengths are always whole numbers), a histogram is not appropriate. However, here is an example of a histogram to represent the birth weights, in grams, of 23 babies.

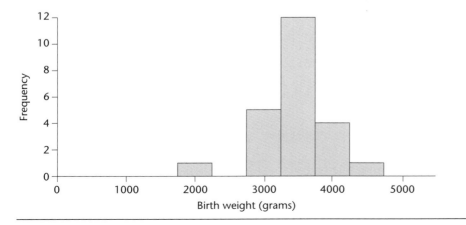

Task 4   Your data: graphing the data

Choose any two of the following which you think might best support your investigation and use them to plot your data:

pie charts, bar charts, pictographs, histograms.

Task 5   Observing data

Examine the different graphs above and make some observations concerning the data. These might concern the most common name lengths, how spread out the name lengths are, and the general distribution of name lengths. You should be able to do these for both the female and male name lengths and also to compare visually the two sets of data.

Comment

Here are some of the observations you might have made:

From the pie charts it is fairly easy to see that most common name length for females is 6, and for males both 4 and 6 are equal first. This shows up in the bar charts as the tallest bar (and is perhaps easier to see here). From the bar charts it can be seen that the spread of name lengths for females is between 4 and 9 and for males between 4 and 11. Less precise observations from the bar charts are that the female name lengths rise to a highest value and then fall away again, whereas the male name lengths are (with the exception of 6) getting fewer as the length of the name increases.

There is another type of very useful graph, a boxplot, which is discussed on pages 63–64.

Graphs give a good visual impression of the data, but we often want more detailed or precise summaries. These need to be found from the data by calculations. The most common sorts of calculation are to find an average (as a measure of a typical value) and to find a measure of how spread out the data are.

Calculating averages

There are three common averages: the mean, mode and median.

The mean

Using a spreadsheet, the function 'AVERAGE' can be used to calculate the mean of a list of numbers.

The **mean** is the most commonly used average and is the one most people are referring to when they say 'the average'. The mean of a list of, say, 15 numbers is calculated by adding the numbers and dividing by 15. For the data on page 56:

Both of the mean values have been rounded to 1 decimal place.

$$\text{Mean female name length} = \frac{5+8+4+...+9+8}{15} = 6.1 \text{ characters}$$

$$\text{Mean male name length} = \frac{8+5+7+...+5+4}{15} = 5.9 \text{ characters}$$

Calculate the mean name lengths of both females and males from your data.

Comment

A useful rough check on whether you calculated the mean correctly is that your answer should lie somewhere between the smallest (minimum) value and the largest (maximum) value of the batch of data. If the calculated mean lies outside this range, it is clearly wrong. Because the mean is found as a result of performing a division calculation, its value will almost always be a decimal number and you must decide to what degree of accuracy to round the answer. The usual convention is to round to one decimal place of accuracy greater than the accuracy of the raw data. In the example given here, the raw data were collected as whole numbers (i.e. zero decimal places) and so the mean was given to one decimal place.

The mode

The **mode** applies to lists of numbers where certain values or categories recur. The mode is the value or category which occurs most frequently. If, say, the heights of twenty people were measured to the nearest millimetre, it is quite possible that everyone would have a different height, in which case the mode could not be used. A way round this problem could be to group the heights into broader bands (perhaps into 2 cm intervals). The mode would then apply to the interval which contained the greatest number of people.

Unlike the mean, the mode need not be restricted to numbers. For example, a company might carry out a survey on how staff travel to work and come up with results like these:

How staff usually travel to work

Car	28
Bus	9
Train	14
Bicycle	19
Walk	16

From this sort of data, only the mode will produce a useful summary – the modal means of transport is the car.

For the female names given on page 56, a name length of 6 is the most common (it occurs five times), so here the mode is 6. For the male name lengths, there are two contenders for the mode, namely 4 and 6 (both occurring four times). In this situation it therefore doesn't make much sense to use the mode.

Task 7	Your data: calculating the mode

Calculate the modes for the female and male name lengths from your data.

Comment

As with the mean, the mode should lie within the range of values contained in the batch. But, unlike the mean, the mode must be one of the members of the batch. So, if the batch consists of whole numbers, the mode must also be a whole number.

The median

The **median** of a batch of numbers is found by sorting the data into order and selecting the middle value.

Spend a moment convincing yourself that the eighth of fifteen values is the middle one.

In the table of sorted names on page 56, there are fifteen numbers in each list so the median is the value of the eighth number when sorted in order. A problem arises where there is an even number of values as there would be no single middle value. For example, suppose there were sixteen numbers in each list. In this case, choose the two middle values, i.e. the eighth and ninth, and the median is the number mid-way between these numbers (i.e. the mean of these numbers).

The eighth female name is 'Marina', with a name length of six characters. So:

median female name length = 6

Similarly, the eighth male name is 'Martin', which also has a name length of six characters. So:

median male name length = 6

Task 8	Your data: calculating the median

Calculate the median female and male name lengths from your data.

Comment

Because your two data batches each consists of an even number of names, after sorting them in order, the median is found by calculating the mean of the two middle values (in your case, the mean of the sixth and seventh values). Like the mean, the median can be applied only to numerical data.

Calculating the spread

Just as there are several ways of measuring averages (the mean, mode and median) there are a number of different measures which show how widely spread the values are. The most common ones are the range, the interquartile range, and the standard deviation. In this section only the first two of these will be covered.

The **range** is the difference between the largest and the smallest value in the batch. For example, the range of female name lengths for the data in the table on page 56 is the length of the longest name (Charlotte) minus the length of the shortest name (Faye), that is $9 - 4 = 5$.

The range of male name lengths is the length of the longest name (Christopher) minus the length of the shortest name (Jack), that is $11 - 4 = 7$.

One problem with the range is that it can easily be affected by an untypical value. For example, if the male names happened to include a Rumpelstiltskin, the range would increase from 7 to 11. One way around this is to measure the range between two values that are not quite at the extremes. The **interquartile range** measures the range of the middle half of the values. It is the difference between the values of the upper quartile and the lower quartile. These two **quartiles** are the values of the numbers that are one-quarter of the way in from either end of the batch once it has been sorted. If there are fifteen values, the **lower quartile** is, roughly speaking, the value of the fourth or fifth number, while the **upper quartile** is, approximately, the value of the eleventh or twelfth number.

It is possible to be more precise than this in defining a quartile but textbooks vary slightly as to how it is defined. It is enough here to know that, in order to find the quartiles, you must first sort the data and then find the two values that are approximately one-quarter of the way in from each end.

The fourth and twelfth values are approximately in the correct position. For the female name lengths for the sorted data in the table on page 56 these are, respectively, 5 and 8, so:

Lower quartile, $Q1 = 5$ and Upper quartile, $Q3 = 8$

Female interquartile range $= Q3 - Q1 = 8 - 5 = 3$

The fourth and twelfth values of the male name lengths for the sorted data are, respectively, 4 and 7, so:

Male interquartile range $= Q3 - Q1 = 7 - 4 = 3$

Your data: calculating the spread   Task 9

Calculate the range and the interquartile ranges of the female and male name lengths from your data.

Boxplots (box and whiskers diagrams)

As was explained earlier, a batch of raw data is difficult to interpret and the summary calculations given above provide an overview of the sort of values it contains. Working from smallest to biggest, five of these summary values are:

minimum value, lower quartile, median, upper quartile, maximum value.

These values can be represented in a type of graph called a **boxplot** (sometimes referred to as a 'box and whiskers' diagram). Overleaf is a boxplot of the name length data:

Boxplots and other novel representations like 'stem and leaf' diagrams were first popularized by John Tukey in America in the 1970s.

The boxplot is a screen picture from a TI-83 graphics calculator.

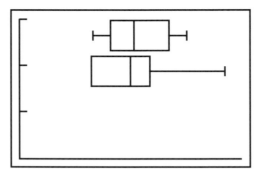

The upper boxplot in the figure shows the five-figure summary of the female name lengths; the lower boxplot corresponds to the male names. The diagram below spells out the positions of each value of a general boxplot.

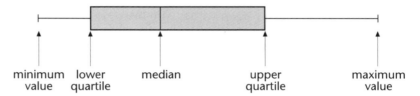

minimum value   lower quartile   median   upper quartile   maximum value

The strength of the boxplot is that it reveals, at a glance, the key features of a batch of data. For example, the central box marks out the interquartile range.

Skew describes data that are bunched to one side with just a few stragglers spread out on the other side.

The lengths of the left and right whiskers indicate how **skewed** the figures are. When two or more boxplots are drawn one below the other on the same scale, direct comparisons can be made between the data batches. For example, from the boxplots of the name lengths you can see that, even though the two medians are equal (both have a value of 6), the middle half of the female name lengths distribution (the central box) contains generally higher values than the middle half of the male name lengths.

Task 10   Your data: drawing a boxplot

Find the minimum value, lower quartile, median, upper quartile, maximum value for each of your data sets and draw boxplots.

Interpreting the results

You have been guided, in turn, through the C and A stages of the name length investigation. At stage A you drew various graphs and performed a variety of summary calculations (finding the mean, mode and median). Not all of these are particularly helpful here, but they were provided in the interests of exploring the range of possible techniques available. In a 'real' investigation, of course, you would probably focus just on those calculations and graphs which might reveal insights into the data. Now you have reached the final I stage where these summaries are interpreted in the light of the question posed in the original problem.

Use the information from your observations on the graphs (Task 5), the boxplots given on page 64 and the three averages to draw some conclusions about whether female name lengths are longer than male name lengths. For convenience, the averages are summarized below.

Mean, mode and median name lengths for females and males

There is no clearly defined mode for male name lengths.

	Mean	Mode	Median
Female names	6.1	6	6
Male names	5.9	–	6

Comment

For female and male name lengths, the medians are equal, whereas the mean length of female names is greater than that of males. So the averages appear to show the same as the graphs, that female names are longer, that there are more short male names. The boxplot appears to confirm this.

Do your data agree with this conclusion?

Can one therefore conclude that, in general, female names are longer? This would be a rash conclusion to make on the basis of the evidence. For a start, the difference between the means is very small: a mere 0.2. Also, the samples were fairly small – only 15 names in each batch. You might be a bit more confident of this conclusion if it had been based on larger sample sizes. To illustrate the point, suppose that, in my search for names in the newspaper, my eye happened to alight on the name Ann instead of Charlotte. Then the mean length of female names would have been 5.7, and so actually smaller than that of the male names.

Knowing which average and graph to use

It is one thing to know how to find the various averages and produce the different graphs, but it is quite another to know when their use is most appropriate. A major problem with learning statistical techniques merely as a set of skills to no real purpose is that appropriateness of use simply doesn't arise. Making an intelligent choice about which to use is most likely to crop up in the context of a real or plausible statistical investigation. This section looks at the pros and cons of the different averages and graphs.

Knowing which average to use

A way of deciding which average to use is to ask: 'Does this average help me to answer my question?' The choice of average will be affected by the precise wording. For example, if you wished to compare 'the length of the typical female name with that of the typical male name', then the median might make the best choice. On the other hand, if you wished to compare 'the most common lengths of the female and male names', you would use the mode.

The next activity will provide you with some contexts in which to practise your skills in choosing an average.

Task 12	Which average?

In a survey, each respondent was asked to record information on a variety of factors. Which average would you choose to summarize the following?

(a) country of origin   (b) lucky number   (c) date of birth

(d) weight   (e) household size

Comment

Example	Preferred average	Comment
(a) country of origin	mode	As the data are non-numerical, only the mode will do.
(b) lucky number	mode	Although these data are numerical, it makes no sense to find the mean or median.
(c) date of birth	mode?	Again, it makes no sense to find the mean or median here. The mode might be useful but only if the data were grouped into months or star sign – it depends on what you want to investigate.
(d) weight	mean, median	Which of these you choose depends on whether you want to know the 'average' weight (the mean) or what a typical person weighs (the median).
(e) household size	median, mode	It would be meaningless to calculate a mean household size of, say 4.7. Choose the median if you want the household size of the average person. Choose the mode if you want the most common household size.

Knowing which graph to use

Like the averages, the graphs are suitable for different purposes and each illustrates some features of the data and ignores others. Before you read on you may like to look over the graphs met so far and make notes of their strengths and weaknesses.

Pie charts

In general, a pie chart is drawn so that the size of each slice matches the number of occurrences of that category. In the pie charts on page 58, the size of each slice of the pie corresponds to the number of people with that particular number of letters in their name.

A pie chart is suitable only for representing a single batch of discrete data. It is also not recommended for numerical data (as has been done here). One reason for this is that having the number categories arranged in a circle is less helpful than if they are arranged on a straight line (you end up with a large number placed alongside a smaller number, which is a bit silly!). Also it can be confusing when trying to represent empty categories (like 9 and 10 letters in the male name lengths, for example). It isn't obvious whether these categories should be represented on the chart or not – there is no room for them on the diagram but the fact should be recorded that there were no occurrences of name lengths between 8 and 11.

On a more positive note, the complete pie actually means something here (it represents all fifteen people in the survey). Don't use a pie chart if the complete pie has no clear meaning. Also, be careful if you are using two pies to represent data from two different-sized batches. The pies should be drawn so that the area of each pie matches its sample size – something that is very difficult to do using a computer! However, in general, pie charts are not very helpful for comparing two batches of data.

Bar charts

Like the pie chart, a bar chart is suitable only for representing discrete data. The bar charts show clearly the pattern of different name lengths and are a good choice here. For example, the tallest bar shows the mode,while the heights of the bars show how frequently the name lengths occurred. Empty categories (for example, 9 and 10 letters in the male name lengths) are represented also – they can be thought of as bars of zero height at positions 9 and 10 on the horizontal axis.

Pictographs

Like the pie chart and bar chart, a pictograph is suitable only for representing discrete data. A pictograph is similar in design to a bar chart except that the quantity in each category is represented by a series of identical drawings (for example, smiling faces). Usually the drawing or picture is chosen to illustrate some feature of the thing being represented. For example, suppose that pupils are keeping track of how many people in their class have used, and have not used, the computer in a particular week.

They might come up with the symbol ⌨ for those who had and the symbol ☹ for those who had not.

A clash of symbols?   Task 13

Suppose that ten people in the class have had their turn at using the class computer and eleven have not.

Why might the following pictograph be misleading?

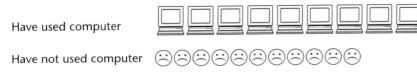

Have used computer

Have not used computer

Comment

Even though there are fewer computer pictures than sad faces, the line of computers is actually longer on the page. The reason for this is that the two icons are not of equal size and are not equally spaced. For a pictograph to convey the right impression, care must be taken with the size and spacing of the pictures.

As was mentioned before, bar charts and pictographs can be drawn with the columns/pictures laid out either vertically or horizontally. Go for the horizontal version if your category labels involve long words or phrases, as is the case in the figure above.

Histograms

Although graphics calculators and computers could draw these data so that adjacent bars were touching, the use of the term 'histogram' here is inappropriate. As mentioned on page 59, histograms are suitable only for depicting continuous data whereas bar charts should be reserved for discrete data.

Investigations using paired data

As was mentioned earlier, the investigation of name lengths enabled you to draw on a range of different calculations and graphs, but two types of graph – the line graph and the scatterplot – were not covered. The reason was that their use was not appropriate for the sort of data that you were using. The line graph and scatterplot are used to represent **paired data** and are useful in investigating relationships between two things.

Line graph

The table below gives the heights of a child taken every year between the ages of 6 and 16 years.

Heights of a child between the ages of 6 and 16 years

Age (years)	6	7	8	9	10	11
Height (cm)	109	111	118	121	125	130
Age (years)	12	13	14	15	16	
Height (cm)	133	148	159	161	161	

This is a line graph depicting the data:

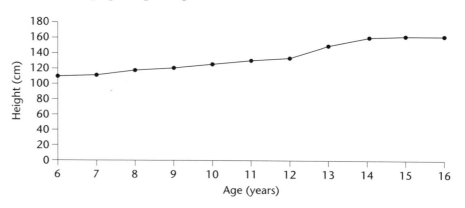

The steeper parts of the graph indicate her growth spurts. The graph levels out at around the age of fourteen or fifteen years when she stopped growing.

Drawing the line graph differently

In drawing line graphs you (or the computer) choose the scales and which values to plot. You may have wondered how much it matters what scales you use and just how you draw the graph. The next task looks at some ways of redrawing the line graph above.

Redrawing the line graph	Task 14

First, you may have noticed that there is a lot of space below a height of 1 metre. Version A below is redrawn so that the vertical axis begins at 100 cm.

Secondly, you may have wondered whether the graph could be drawn with the two axes interchanged. This is version B.

Thirdly, the horizontal scale has been squashed up. This is version C.

Do these three versions seem valid ways of representing the data? If not, why not?

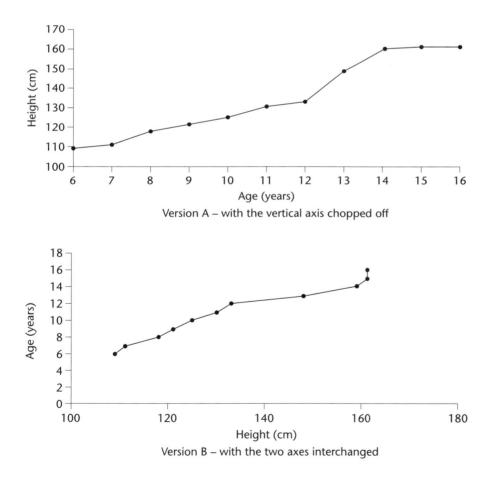

Version A – with the vertical axis chopped off

Version B – with the two axes interchanged

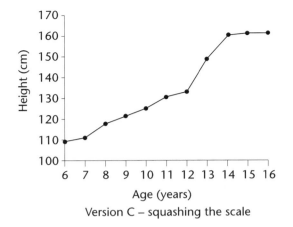

Version C – squashing the scale

Comment

Version A: There is no problem with chopping the vertical or horizontal axes but, if possible, it is a good idea to indicate that you have done so by drawing a little break in the axis, as shown here:

However, this is difficult to achieve using graphs drawn on computer, so the reader needs to check carefully the scales on both axes.

Version B: Unfortunately, this is simply wrong.

There may be situations where it is not clear which is dependent on which; in such cases it probably doesn't matter too much!

An agreed convention when drawing graphs of paired data is that the 'independent' variable is placed on the horizontal axis and the 'dependent' variable on the vertical axis. A way of deciding which is which is to say to yourself: 'Does a child's height depend on her age, or does her age depend on her height?' Clearly the answer is the former, and so the dependent variable Height should be placed on the vertical axis. If Time is a variable, it is usually placed on the horizontal axis.

Version C: This graph is actually correct, but notice how this squashing changes the slope of the line. Beware of jumping to conclusions if a graph appears to rise or fall very steeply. This effect can be created artificially by chopping the vertical axis or altering the scales.

Bar chart or line graph?

If the data being displayed are discrete (i.e. are either discrete numbers or categories) drawing a chart where the values are joined up as a line graph is inappropriate. In general, line graphs are used to represent continuous data. Only join up the values on a graph if the lines between the points make sense. The two graphs below, showing a survey of pets in a primary school class, illustrate this.

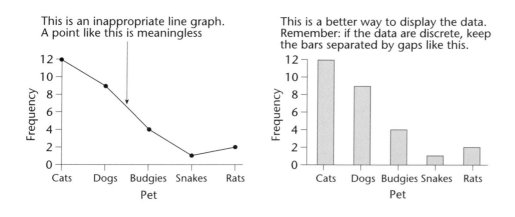

This is an inappropriate line graph.
A point like this is meaningless

This is a better way to display the data.
Remember: if the data are discrete, keep
the bars separated by gaps like this.

Scatterplot

In a psychological experiment, a volunteer, Irene, was shown photographs of 25 people of widely varying ages and asked to guess the age of each person. The researcher then used a **scatterplot**, plotting Irene's guesses on the vertical axis and the actual ages on the horizontal axis. This is shown below.

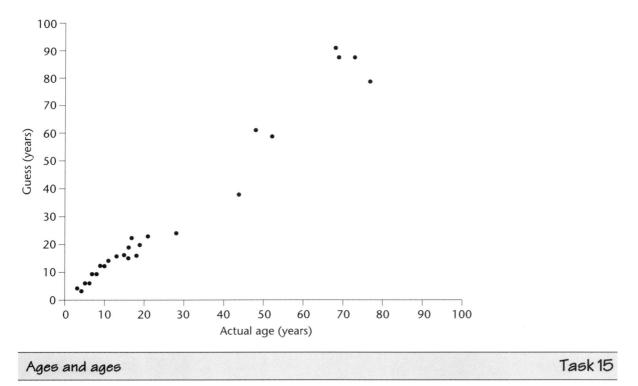

| Ages and ages | Task 15 |

(a) Describe the main features of this scatterplot.

(b) What does it tell you about the relationship between the two variables in question?

Comment

The points lie in roughly a straight line, running from bottom left to top right of the graph. In other words, the higher the actual age, the higher was Irene's guess. There is therefore a positive relationship between the two variables.

The pattern of points suggests that her guesses were quite good. Imagine a straight line drawn from the origin (i.e. the point with Actual age = 0 and Guess = 0) to the point with Actual age = 80 and Guess = 80. Such a line goes through all points where the guess was the same as the actual age and therefore represents a set of perfect guesses. A measure of how good Irene's guesses were is to see how far the crosses on the scatterplot lie from this imaginary line. Also, you can see at a glance whether Irene has a tendency to over-estimate (indicated by points above the line) or under-estimate (points below the line).

Further reading

Centre for Mathematics Education, The Open University (1994) *An ABC of Number (M520)*, The Open University.

Alan Graham and David Green (1994) *Data Handling*, *Practical Guide Series*, Scholastic Publications.

Alan Graham (1994) *Teach Yourself Statistics*, Hodder and Stoughton.

4. Number and algebra

Introduction

For many people, the word 'algebra' conjures up a forest of letters, numbers and symbols, and a memory of apparently pointless rules for doing things with expressions and solving equations. This is similar to having the impression that cooking is only about following complicated recipes using special techniques. It misses the point about algebra, its power and simplicity.

Algebra is about generalized mathematical thinking arising from seeing patterns and relationships. It is about expressing those patterns in words, symbols, diagrams and graphs, and interpreting what is observed. The important patterns are ones that are not just particular to one situation, but are generalizations that apply to many different situations that have underlying similarities. Expressing these perceived generalities is the root of algebra, which is why algebra is also concerned with:

> 'Algebra is an attribute, a fundamental power of the mind. Not of mathematics only.' (Gattegno, 1977)

▶ expressing the same thing in different forms;

▶ 'doing and undoing'.

This section is in five main parts, all of which are aspects of algebra:

▶ *finding and using pattern* – saying and recording what is seen in different ways;

▶ *generalized arithmetic* – becoming explicitly aware of the rules for manipulating numbers;

▶ *finding the unknown* – using a symbol to stand for an as-yet-unknown quantity, which can be used to form and solve equations;

▶ *using formulas* – formulas as shorthand, and using them to find values;

▶ *picturing functions* – representing functions as equations, tables and graphs.

Finding and using pattern

Generality is an important part of mathematics. Its most basic and clear instance is in pattern spotting, in seeing links and connections between things. This section takes a simple situation and uses it to demonstrate several of the processes of algebraic thinking, including becoming aware of a pattern and expressing it in words, pictures and symbols.

Identifying and expressing generality

Although we often talk about 'seeing' a pattern, visualizing a pattern in your head is not the only way of being aware of it. You may find a pattern more obvious when spoken; or you may prefer to draw diagrams or use words and symbols. These are all important ways of expressing patterns and you can improve your algebraic thinking by being able to move between them. The following tasks are designed to help you gain confidence in doing this.

In the first block below, shade in every third circle starting from the second, counting left to right, row by row.

○ ○
○ ○
○ ○
○ ○
○ ○
○ ○
○ ○
○ ○
○ ○
○ ○
○ ○
○ ○
○ ○

Comment

Many people find that at some point they shift from counting to following a pattern. At first, they are not confident of the pattern, and so keep counting, but then the pattern takes over. If you did not notice this happening, try another version on the second block: shade in every fifth circle starting from the third.

On a fresh block, shade in every third circle starting from the second, but this time counting from left to right in the first row, then right to left in the second, and so on, weaving your way down the rows. Look out for when your brain moves from counting to having confidence in the pattern. Try to say what happened.

Comment

These tasks illustrate the power we all have for seeking out and employing patterns. The tasks started with a given counting rule, 'shade in every …' but in doing the task the brain simplified it to something like 'lines are developing' and 'just continue the lines …'.

Tasks 1 and 2 were concerned with *seeing* a pattern. To reach generality you need to be able to *express* a pattern in words and symbols. How you do this is closely connected with the way in which you see the pattern. The following tasks take you through the process of expressing generality arising from a sequence of diagrams.

Imagine a brick wall being built. The sequence of pictures below show stages in building a two-layer wall.

Notice what is happening in the sequence of bricks and describe to yourself how the sequence is being built up.

Comment

Here are three of the many different ways of 'seeing' and 'saying' the brick sequence.

The pictures have become two-dimensional because they are easier to draw yet retain the pattern.

'One brick, and then one brick with one pair of bricks added on, then one with two pairs added on, one with three pairs added on, …'

'There are two rows, the top row having one brick less than the bottom row. The bottom row has one, two, three, … bricks in it, … The number on the bottom is the same as its position in the sequence.'

'One brick, three bricks, five bricks, seven bricks, … This fits the odd numbers, and is going up in twos.'

To be confident that you can express the generality here, it is not enough to 'see and say' the pattern. You need to be able to express how to find the number of bricks in any given stage in the sequence. To test that you can do this you need to pick a stage in the sequence; then use your way of seeing to work out how many bricks there are at that stage. You need to choose a particular number, but one that isn't too special: here we choose 37.

This is an instance of specializing.

Each way of seeing and saying gives rise to a particular method of finding the number of bricks. You could draw the whole sequence from 1 to 37 adding two bricks each time and then counting the bricks in the 37th picture, but that would give you no insight into the generality (and would take a long time). You are looking for a more concise version which reflects the way in which you see the sequence.

Task 4	Number 37

Choose one of the ways of 'seeing and saying' the brick pattern, and use it to work out the 37th in the sequence. How many bricks would there be?

Comment

Taking the second way of seeing you might produce something like:

> Picture number 37 in the sequence will have two rows of bricks. There will be 37 bricks in the bottom row, and one less (36) bricks in the top row – so there are 73 altogether.

This could be shortened to:

> Picture 37 needs 37 (bottom row) + 36 (top row) bricks, so 73 altogether.

Algebraic thinking has already begun.

See Learning and doing, pages 5–6.

Alternatively, if you had recalled the connection with the sequence of odd numbers worked on in the Learning and doing section, you might have remembered (or looked up) that the nth odd number is $2n - 1$, so the 37th is:

$$2 \times 37 - 1 = 74 - 1, \text{ making 73 bricks.}$$

Task 5	How many bricks?

Using the same brick sequence as above, I have a 'picture number' in my head. Say out loud how to calculate the number of bricks in the picture.

This question is the heart of the 'expressing generality' aspect of algebra.

Now try to write down the instructions. How will you convince yourself that your solution works?

Comment

You probably said something like:

> Whatever 'picture number' you are thinking of, add it to one less than it.

You may have felt that producing a general statement was more challenging than producing the 37th number, because of the difficulty of finding a way of referring to an unknown number. You may even have felt that you could have used symbols.

Recording in different forms

When starting to record algebra symbolically some people like to refer to the unknown by drawing a little cloud ☁ or 'thinks bubble' for 'the number in your head', or □, to indicate a box into which the number can be put. Others do not find clouds or boxes helpful, and prefer words, such as 'picture number', or letters, such as p. Using letters is certainly neither obvious nor automatic; using clouds or empty boxes may provide a stronger image of an as-yet-unknown.

The following are some ways of recording the number of bricks in a general picture in the brick sequence:

▶ The number of bricks in any brick picture is the total of the picture number and one less than the picture number.

▶ Number of bricks = ☁ add ☁ take away 1

▶ Number of bricks = ☐ plus ☐ less 1

▶ Number of bricks = (picture number) plus (picture number - 1)

▶ Number of bricks = $p + (p - 1)$ which is the same as $2p - 1$

Each of these statements says the same thing; and they each have strengths and weaknesses.

Different forms of recording   **Task 6**

Think about the advantages and disadvantages of each of the above methods of recording the number of bricks in a general picture.

Comment

The word statement retains the meaning but its wordiness may make it difficult to follow. The statements using symbols are shorter to write but drawing the pictures is a bit laborious. The expression using p is succinct and so easy to write, but because it is so concise it may need more interpreting. It does have one very important advantage: it is the easiest to simplify. The expression $p + (p - 1)$ simplifies to $2p - 1$, which gives an even more concise form.

$p + p$ is 'two p' which is written as $2p$.

The instructions for calculating the number of bricks could be written as a mathematical formula:

$$b = 2p - 1$$

where b is the number of bricks and p is the picture number in the sequence.

The steps in generating a rule for a sequence can be summarized as follows.

▶ Say how you see the pattern continuing, and try to identify other ways of seeing it.

▶ For each way of seeing, state a rule or method for generating the sequence.

▶ Decide how a general picture can be built, and use it to find a systematic way of counting.

▶ Express your way of counting, perhaps first in pictures or words, then in some shortened form, perhaps as a mathematical formula.

Look at the following sequences of numbers. In each case predict the value of the next three **terms** (numbers).

(a) 3, 6, 9, 12, ...   (b) 4, 7, 10, 13, ...

Then try to work out the general rule for the value of the nth term.

Comment

(a) 15, 18, 21
   You should have noticed that the numbers given are the start of the 3 times table. So the value of the nth term will be 3n.

(b) 16, 19, 22
   Each term is one more than those in the previous example, so the nth term would be 3n +1, but do not be concerned if you did not work this out for yourself. Some other ways of getting to 'see the pattern' are shown below.

A word of caution here. Not enough information was given in Task 7 to be absolutely sure what the next three numbers were. You needed to assume that there was some underlying numerical rule. If not, then the next three numbers might be almost anything. Slightly ridiculous examples will illustrate this: suppose the numbers came from buses arriving at a bus stop, lottery numbers, or ages of children in a family. No sequence is unique unless a rule is given.

Generalized arithmetic

Algebra is probably most often thought of as generalized arithmetic – you do to the letters what you usually do to the numbers. But this only makes sense if you already know what it is that you do to numbers! You need to be able to attend to how you do computations rather than just to what the answer is. It is not at all easy to describe in words what you do, but struggling to express it is important in the development of your mathematical thinking. This process takes considerable practice and experience, and so it is well worth working on at every opportunity.

Look at this:

$$(3 \times 4 + 8) \div 5$$

This expression can be seen in two ways:

▸ as a set of instructions for calculating;

▸ as a number, 4, the result of carrying out the calculation.

This dual aspect of an expression – as procedure and as answer – is central to algebraic thinking. This section concentrates on the first of them.

4 + 5 =   5 + 4 =

Notice that you get the same answer to both of the calculations shown.

Does this always work? How might you express it more generally?

Comment

Letting F stand for 'First number', and S for 'Second number', you could express the generality illustrated by $4 + 5 = 5 + 4$ as $F + S = S + F$.

Here you need to shift your attention from what kinds of calculations you can do (like adding, subtracting, etc.), to what properties those calculations have. For example, $4 + 5$ equals $5 + 4$ not just because they both have the answer 9, but because it does not matter in which order you do the calculation. The underlying rule is a rule of arithmetic, and also a rule for manipulating algebraic symbols.

Properties of operations

This section looks at the underlying properties of the operations of arithmetic. There are several different properties, which you probably often use without really thinking about them. Being aware of them will enable you to use them more consciously and effectively, as well as deepening your understanding of number.

Work these out mentally:

(a) $7 + 8 + 3 + 2$ (b) $5 \times 13 \times 2$

(c) $53 - 28 + 7 - 2$ (d) $7 + 95$

Think about how you did the calculations. Did you find any shortcuts? Can you see any quick ways of doing them now?

Comment

The answers do not matter, what is important here are the methods. The quick methods all involve carrying out the calculations in a different order to the way they are written. In (a) it is much quicker to work out $7 + 3$ and $8 + 2$ and then add the results. Similar strategies work in parts (b) and (c). In part (d) many people reverse the sum and start with 95 and add 7 to it (you possibly did not even notice yourself doing it). The methods for (a) and (d) work because it does not matter what order you add numbers together nor which additions you carry out first. That is true for multiplication also.

These properties all have formal names. Although you will need to be able to recognize the names, it is more important to have a grasp of what the properties are.

With these calculation shortcuts you make use of some of the properties of the number system. In order to understand the significance of these properties they need to be separated.

Order. With multiplication and addition, the order does not matter. In the sum $7 + 95$, the answer comes out the same when the numbers are reversed to $95 + 7$. Similarly $7 \times 5 = 5 \times 7$.

An operation which can be carried out in any order is called **commutative**. As you will see, this property does not hold for subtraction or division.

This is quite different from ordinary language, where for example, 'dead butterfly collector' has two different meanings, depending on which words are paired (a hyphen is used).

Pairing. When you add $13 + 8 + 2$, it does not matter if you first add the 13 and 8 together and then add 2, or if you first add 8 and 2 to get 10 and then work out 13 add 10. This can be shown using brackets:

$$13 + 8 + 2 = (13 + 8) + 2$$
$$\text{or} \quad 13 + 8 + 2 = 13 + (8 + 2)$$

Notice that the order of the numbers is the same, it is the pairing that changes. An operation in which the pairing does not matter is called **associative**.

These two properties are now discussed in more detail.

The commutative property: order does not matter

In Task 9, $7 + 95$ was changed to $95 + 7$. This is possible for any type of number. The operations of addition and multiplication are commutative. Written in mathematical shorthand:

$$a + b = b + a \quad \text{and} \quad a \times b = b \times a$$

where a and b could be integers, fractions, or any other kind of number, or even an algebraic expression.

However, the order in which calculations are carried out *does* matter with other operations.

Task 10	Commutative

Are subtraction and division commutative? Try some examples.

Comment

Neither subtraction nor division are commutative: the order of the numbers matters. For example:

$$5 - 2 = 3 \text{ but } 2 - 5 = {}^-3$$
$$6 \div 3 = 2 \text{ but } 3 \div 6 = \tfrac{1}{2}$$

Notice that it is only necessary to have one **counter-example** of each to show that subtraction and division are not commutative.

The associative property: pairing does not matter

$$13 + 8 + 2 = (13 + 8) + 2 = 13 + (8 + 2)$$

Again, this holds for any type of number. The operation of addition is associative:

$$(a + b) + c = a + (b + c)$$

Replace the symbol ∘ in:

   8 ∘ 4 ∘ 2

by ×, − and ÷ in turn. Pair off each in two different ways, using brackets, and see whether the answers are different.

Which of subtraction, multiplication and division are associative and which are not?

Comment

Multiplication is associative, but subtraction and division are not. For example:

   $(8 − 4) − 2 = 4 − 2 = 2$ but $8 − (4 − 2) = 8 − 2 = 6$

so $(8 − 4) − 2 \neq 8 − (4 − 2)$

$\neq$ is the symbol for 'is not equal to'.

Mixing addition and multiplication

The two properties discussed so far are sufficient to be able to change the order and pairings in any calculation involving just addition or just multiplication. Calculations which involve a mixture of addition and multiplication often make use of another property, the distributive property. This is explained through looking at the method of long multiplication.

Work through the multiplication of 37 by 19 using your own preferred written method and then list the individual calculations of which it comprises (even if you do some of them in your head).

Comment

There are many ways of doing the calculation, but one common method of long multiplication is analysed below (this may be different to the way you 'see' it, so be prepared to work through it slowly):

   37
   19 Think of 19 as (10 + 9).
   370 (10 × 37)
   333 (9 × 37)
   703 (10 × 37) + (9 × 37)

It is perhaps not surprising that few children understand this method and most have to practise it many times before being able do it.

Writing this method another way:

   $37 × 19 = 37 × (10 + 9) = (37 × 10) + (37 × 9)$

This property is known as the **distributive law** of multiplication over addition. Written out in general form it is:

   $a × (b + c) = (a × b) + (a × c)$

'5' and '6' can be replaced by any numbers, of course.

Although this expression looks daunting, its meaning is almost obvious. Informally it says:

> 5 lots of something and 6 lots of something are equal to 11 lots of something.

Visually, seeing the numbers as arrays of dots, the long multiplication method for 37×19 is:

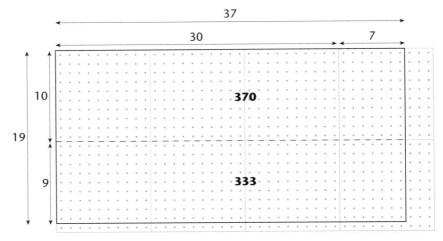

The more abstract form, $a \times (b + c) = (a \times b) + (a \times c)$, can be represented by a similar diagram:

$$a \times (b+c) = a \times b + a \times c$$
$$= ab + ac$$

This property is used for multiplying algebraic expressions as well as numbers, so:

$$3(x + y) = 3x + 3y$$

There is an equivalent property for subtraction:

$$a \times (b - c) = (a \times b) - (a \times c)$$

Task 13	Reflection

You may find this difficult; but the process of thinking about both notions of algebra will help you to reflect on your learning so far.

What links do you see between the notions of expressing generality in patterns and generalized arithmetic? Try thinking about what is the same and what is different.

Comment

When asked this question one learner came up with the following:

> In both, letters are used to represent numbers. In expressing generality, letters are combined to make a pattern stand out, to make a relationship obvious so it can be used as a rule for calculating outputs from inputs. In generalized arithmetic the letters are used to highlight a statement that is always true whatever kind of number or expression the letters represent.

Equations – finding the unknown

Think back to a time in the past when you encountered equations (or a particular equation), and recall any memories that you have. This may involve thinking back a number of years to when you were taught equations at school or recalling any moment in your life where the idea of an equation was relevant.

You may find that the following sorts of things come to mind:

> Equations are things you have to solve to find x.
> You have to balance the left- and right-hand sides.
> Whatever you do to one side, you must do to the other.
> You have to find the missing number.
> Change the side, change the sign.
> Find the value of x.
> There are simultaneous equations that have both x and y.

Most of these statements involve equations as things to be acted upon and on the methods or techniques that are often taught. This section revisits the topic of equations and will try to give you a perspective on equations which is not simply about methods for solving them.

The most usual methods taught in schools to solve equations are based on algebra. This is mainly because, when such methods are possible, they give exact answers. This section concentrates on the use of algebra.

In science and engineering and other areas where mathematics is used frequently, many equations are solved by using graphs or by putting in numerical values. See page 96.

What is an equation?   **Task 14**

Look through this list of statements and decide which ones you would consider to be equations and which ones you wouldn't:

$$7 + 3 = 10 \qquad 2x - 1 = 29 \qquad V = IR$$

$$(y - 3)(y + 4) \qquad 2x + 3 = x + 1 \qquad ax + by + c = 0$$

$$x + y = 10 \qquad 4a = a + a + a + a \qquad x = 5$$

Comment

There is no single 'right' definition of an equation. All equations have an equals sign and most involve some algebraic expression. People disagree, for instance, about whether a letter has to be present or whether an equation can consist only of letters, as in $V = IR$.

Mary's husband George is known for Boolean algebra: the logic used by computers.

Mary Boole (1832–1916) was an influential mathematics teacher and educator. Her writings are full of wise observations which are remarkably modern in their perceptiveness and expression. Possibly her most famous observation is as follows.

> When people had only arithmetic and not algebra, they found out a surprising amount of things about numbers and quantities. But there remained problems which they very much needed to solve and could not. They had to guess the answer; and, of course, they usually guessed wrong [...] At last (at least I should suppose this is what happened) some man, or perhaps some woman, suddenly said: 'How stupid we've all been! We have been dealing logically with all the facts we knew about this problem, except the most important fact of all, the fact of our own ignorance. Let us include that among the facts we have to be logical about, and see where we get to then. In this problem besides the numbers which we do know, there is one we do not know. Instead of guessing whether we are to call it none, or seven, or a hundred and twenty, or a thousand and fifty, let us agree to call it x, and let us always remember that x stands for the Unknown. Let us write x in among all our other numbers, and deal logically with it according to exactly the same laws as we deal with six or nine or a hundred or a thousand.'

Mary Boole's notion of acknowledging ignorance comes into its own in tasks like the following, the kind of problems which many people associate with algebra.

Think of a number

Look at these 'think of a number' problems:

- I have a number in mind. I double it, add 3 and the answer is 131. What's my number?

- I have a number in my mind. I subtract 1 and multiply by 3, then subtract 7 and the answer is 8. What's my number?

These questions correspond to equations, the first to $2x + 3 = 131$, the second to $3(x - 1) - 7 = 8$. The fact that word puzzles like these can be written as equations gives a way of thinking about equations. When these equations are treated like number problems, you can use an informal method of solving them. This method may be called 'working backwards' or 'undoing'. For example, on the first of the problems:

> If the number has been doubled and then 3 added to give a result of 131, then before the 3 was added, it had to be 128 (3 less than 131).

> So, a number has been doubled to give 128, therefore the original number is 64 (half of 128).

A picture, such as the one below, perhaps shows more clearly the 'undoing' or 'working backwards' nature of this method.

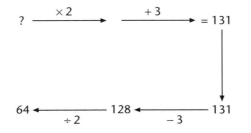

Take the second of the 'think of a number' problems above and find the solution by working backwards, either by drawing a diagram or writing.

Comment

The diagram looks like this:

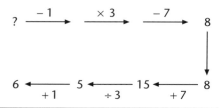

To use 'think of a number' problems as a means of solving equations you need to be able to translate between the words and the equation. You need to be able to carry out this translating both ways. Here is the translation of the second 'think of a number' problem:

I have a number in my mind.	x
I subtract 1 ...	$x - 1$
and multiply by 3, ...	$3(x - 1)$
then subtract 7 ...	$3(x - 1) - 7$
and the answer is 8.	$3(x - 1) - 7 = 8$

Note the use of brackets to show the order of operations.

The solution to this equation can be carried out in exactly the same way as the original problem.

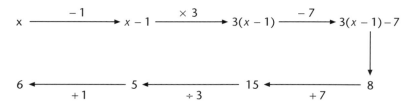

Translate these equations and number problems into the other form.

(a) I am thinking of a number. I subtract 5, multiply by 2, add 4 and the answer is 12. What is my number?

(b) I am thinking of a number. I add 7, multiply by 2, subtract 10 and finally divide by 5. The result is 2. What was my original number?

(c) $2x + 4 = 12$

(d) $2\left(\dfrac{x}{3} - 5\right) + 4 = 12$

Comment

The answers are:

(a) $2(x - 5) + 4 = 12$

(b) $\dfrac{2(x + 7) - 10}{5} = 2$

(c) I am thinking of a number. I multiply by 2, add 4 and the answer is 12. What is my number?

(d) I am thinking of a number. I divide by 3, subtract 5, multiply by 2, add 4 and the answer is 12. What is my number?

You could solve these by the 'undoing' method, and check the answers by fitting them into the original equations.

Pairs of equations

This concerns the topic often called **simultaneous equations**.

When you were asked to think about what an equation is, one of the expressions given was:

$$x + y = 10$$

This has an equal sign and algebraic symbols, but differs from the equations just considered because it has two unknowns and expresses a relationship between them. It could be translated into a 'think of a number' problem:

I'm thinking of two numbers which add to 10.

There is no single 'solution' to this equation, but infinitely many pairs of numbers that fit. Here are some of them:

$x = 3, y = 7$
$x = 9, y = 1$
$x = {}^-3, y = 13$
$x = 1.6, y = 8.4$
$x = 110, y = {}^-100$

Now a second clue is given:

The two numbers also differ by 4.

Translated into an algebraic equation, this becomes:

$$x - y = 4$$

Task 17　　　　　Two clues

(a) Find the numbers which both fit the two clues:

I'm thinking of two numbers which add to 10.
The two numbers also differ by 4.

(b) What are the two numbers if they differ by 6 instead of by 4? by 2? by 8? by 12? by 7? Trying all of these should give you a sense of how the values of the two numbers change as the condition alters. Make up some more if you are still not confident.

(c) Try some others:

    (i)   I'm thinking of two numbers which add to 12. The two numbers also differ by 4.

    (ii)   I'm thinking of two numbers which add to 100. The two numbers also differ by 36.

(d) Make up similar problems for yourself.

Remember that being able to make up suitable examples is a good way of assessing how much you understand.

Comment

Such questions as these are self-checking. If the two numbers fit the initial conditions, then they must be the correct values. What is important here is that you develop some awareness of how the numbers depend on the condition and develop some informal methods of finding the numbers.

You might wonder whether there is any value in expressing such problems in algebra rather than words. Algebra is briefer, but perhaps not as easy to understand. There *is* an advantage in symbols as the following shows.

Consider the two clues:

I'm thinking of two numbers which add to 8.
I double the first number and add the second to get 14.

Expressed in symbols these clues are:

$x + y = 8$
$2x + y = 14$

Looking at the left-hand sides of these equations it is easy to see that the bottom one has an extra x. This x must be equal to the increase on the right-hand side, 6 (= 14 − 8). So $x = 6$ and, because x and y add to 8, $y = 2$.

Notice what was involved here. You need to think about what the equations *mean*, and to be able to move between the symbols and numbers.

Pairs of equations   Task 18

Find the solutions to the following pairs of equations.

(a) $4x + y = 44$
     $x + y = 20$

(b) $4x + 3y = 247$
     $4x − y = 83$

(c) $6x + y = 90$
     $3x − y = 9$

Comment

The answers are self-checking (the numbers must fit *both* equations). In part (c), when you compare the two equations, you get another equation with both x and y in it ($3x + 2y = 81$). This seems to leave you no better off, but if you then compare this with the second of the equations, you will be able to get the value for y.

Inequalities

So far you have been dealing with equations and using the equals sign. In everyday life you are more likely to meet situations which have a range of solutions and use phrases such as 'more than' or 'fewer than' or their equivalent. These expression are called **inequalities** and the symbols used for their shorthand are:

Musicians use similar symbols: an elongated < for crescendo (quiet to loud) and > for diminuendo (from loud to quiet).

$<$, meaning 'fewer than' or 'less than' or 'smaller than', as in $3 < 7$ [smaller < larger];

$\leq$, meaning 'less than or equal to';

$>$, meaning 'greater than', 'more than', 'larger than', as in $7 > 3$ [larger > smaller];

$\geq$, meaning 'greater than or equal to'.

When you buy car insurance there are several variables to consider, such as the type of car that is to be insured, the place where it will be kept and details of the driver including age. The way ages are grouped or categorized is not always clear. For example a 'young driver' could be described as being aged 17 to 24. How do you interpret this? If you have had your 24th birthday recently, you may wonder whether this includes you or not. If you know that the next group is listed as 25 to 29 then this may help, but in mathematics, sets need to be defined precisely. This can be done in symbols or diagrams.

For example 'aged 17 to 24' includes all ages from 17 (including 17 exactly) to all those who are 24 but not yet 25:

$17 \leq$ age of driver < 25

or if we call the age a, then:

$17 \leq a < 25$

Pictures are also used for inequalities, with a filled circle to show that the value can be included and an empty circle to show it cannot. For example:

●————————————○
17   25

Task 19	Interpreting

How would you interpret the following?

(a) ●————————————○
    30   49

(b) $a \geq 50$

(c) $17 < x < 65$

Comment

(a) 30 to 49 (but not yet 49)

(b) 50 or over

(c) x is greater than 17 and less than 65, so between 17 and 65 (for example, 36 or 41.5).

Formulas

These are some formulas that you may have met:

The area of a triangle (b = base, h = height):

$$A = \tfrac{1}{2}bh$$

Changing Fahrenheit (°F) temperatures into Celsius (°C):

$$C = \tfrac{5}{9}(F - 32)$$

Connecting distance, time and speed:

$$\text{speed} = \frac{\text{distance}}{\text{time}}$$

The circumference of a circle (r = radius):

$$C = 2\pi r$$

Einstein's equation (e = energy, m = mass, c is the speed of light):

$$e = mc^2$$

Formulas are used a great deal outside of mathematics classrooms, usually as a set of instructions for calculating. They mostly relate to some specific relationship, rather than being an abstract equation. Even so, they are really just a particular kind of equation and so can be used and manipulated in the same way as equations.

One of the formulas above is for converting temperatures in degrees Fahrenheit to degrees Celsius. Written in words it says:

Take the Fahrenheit temperature and subtract 32; multiply the result by 5 and divide by 9 (or, otherwise, multiply by $\tfrac{5}{9}$).

There has been a shift over the years in the plural for 'formula'. In older books it was written 'formulæ', then 'formulae' became standard, and now 'formulas' is the most used plural.

Words for formulas   Task 20

Write each of the formulas above in words, suitable for carrying out a calculation.

Comment

Suitable forms are as follows (yours may differ slightly):

Area of a triangle: take the length of the base, multiply it by the height and divide by 2.

Speed: divide distance by time.

The circumference of a circle: multiply the radius by pi and then by 2.

Energy: multiply the speed of light by itself and then by the mass.

Substituting in formulas

Putting numbers in formulas is straightforward if the formula is designed to give you exactly the information you want. Sometimes the formula is arranged 'the wrong way'. For example, you may want to convert from °C

to °F but the formula

$$C = \tfrac{5}{9}(F - 32)$$

converts the other way.

Task 21	Substituting in formulas

Formulas normally refer to quantities and so often care has to be taken with the units of measure, particularly with compound measures, such as mph.

Use the formulas above to find these values:

(a) the area of a triangle with base 5 cm and height 12 cm;

(b) the Celsius temperature corresponding to 80 °F;

(c) the distance covered at a speed of 43 km/hour for 1.3 hours;

(d) the height of a triangle, whose base is 3.2 cm and whose area is 14.7 cm².

Comment

The answers to these are:

(a) 30 cm²   (b) 26.7 °C   (c) 55.9 km   (d) 9.19 cm

The temperature and height are given to 3 significant figures.

While the first two of these involve straightforward substitution into the formulas, the others are more tricky, since the formula in each case is written 'the wrong way round'.

There are two ways of dealing with this difficulty in substituting. The first method is simply to put the numbers in the formula and then see what you have to do to find the answer. So, with the part (d) above, putting in the numbers gives:

$$14.7 = \tfrac{1}{2} \times 3.2 \times h$$

This simplifies to $14.7 = 1.6 \times h$, and so h can then be found as $14.7 \div 1.6$.

This method often works quite well, but if you have several calculations to carry out the wrong way round, it is often quicker to re-arrange the formula, and use the new one. There are various methods for re-arranging formulas, but the one you are most likely to need is the 'undoing' method, which was used with equations.

As an example, look again at the formula for converting temperatures in degrees Fahrenheit to degrees Celsius:

$$C = \tfrac{5}{9}(F - 32)$$

Drawing this as a diagram produces:

$$F \xrightarrow{-32} F - 32 \xrightarrow{\times 5} 5(F - 32) \xrightarrow{\div 9} \tfrac{5}{9}(F - 32)$$

Undoing, and putting in the formulas as you do so, produces:

$$F \xrightarrow{-32} F - 32 \xrightarrow{\times 5} 5(F - 32) \xrightarrow{\div 9} \tfrac{5}{9}(F - 32)$$

$$F = \tfrac{9C}{5} + 32 \xleftarrow{+32} \tfrac{9C}{5} \xleftarrow{\div 5} 9C \xleftarrow{\times 9} C$$

This gives the formula:

$$F = \frac{9C}{5} + 32$$

The important feature to notice in producing the diagram is that you need to start with the symbol that you wish to make the 'subject' of the formula. In this case there were only the two symbols C and F, but in the formula for the area of a triangle:

$$A = \tfrac{1}{2}bh$$

there are three symbols.

Re-arranging formulas   Task 22

Re-arrange the following formulas using the 'doing and undoing' method.

(a) The area of a triangle, $A = \tfrac{1}{2}bh$, to give a formula for the height.

(b) speed $= \dfrac{\text{distance}}{\text{time}}$ to give a formula for (i) distance and (ii) time.

(c) The circumference of a circle, $C = 2\pi r$, to give a formula for the radius.

(d) Einstein's equation, $e = mc^2$, to give a formula for c, the speed of light.

Comment

The answers are:

(a) $h = \dfrac{2A}{b}$

(b) (i) distance = speed × time   (ii) time $= \dfrac{\text{distance}}{\text{speed}}$

(c) $r = \dfrac{C}{2\pi}$ (d) $c = \sqrt{\dfrac{e}{m}}$

Square root 'undoes' squaring.

Picturing functions

Several of the formulas you have met so far concern the relationship between two quantities. For example:

▶ The formula $C = \frac{5}{9}(F - 32)$ for converting degrees Fahrenheit to degrees Celsius shows a relationship between C and F. To any value of F there will be a corresponding value of C.

▶ In the brick and picture example, the general formula $b = 2p - 1$ shows the relationship between b for the number of bricks and p for the picture number.

Relationships like these between two quantities are called **functions**. The formulas can be thought of as 'machines' which enable you to find the values corresponding to any number input. The formulas are a particularly useful way of representing a function when you want to find values, but do not reveal all the aspects of the relationship clearly. Functions can also be represented by tables and graphs, which emphasize different features and allow you to see other properties of the relationship.

In this section the connection between formulas, tables and graphs will be explored, including the use of graphs to solve equations. To keep matters simple, all of the functions will be written in a standard form. So, for example, the Fahrenheit and Celsius function will be written as:

$$y = \frac{5}{9}(x - 32)$$

The point of this is to enable you to tell at a glance which part of the function formula is being referred to.

and the brick picture function as:

$$y = 2x - 1$$

Tables for functions

Tables are useful to get a feel for the values involved in a function and for drawing a graph if you need to do it by hand. Take the function $y = 3x + 1$. Values of this function can be shown in a table:

x	0	1	2	3	4	5	6	...
$y = 3x + 1$	1	4	7	10	13	16	19	...

Task 23	Looking across and down

Look along the y row of the table. Write down what you notice.

Now look down each column to see the $3x + 1$ pattern.

Comment

The top row increases by one each time; the bottom row increases by 3. Or, put another way, there is a difference of 3 between adjacent numbers in the bottom row.

Reading down the columns in the table, the numbers can be written as **ordered pairs** (x, y):

$(0, 1),\ (1, 4),\ (2, 7),\ (3, 10), (4, 13), \ldots$

In each ordered pair, the second number is always

$3 \times$ (the first number) + 1

These ordered pairs can then be plotted as points on a graph. The first value (the x value) is always on the horizontal axis.

Plotting a graph	Task 24

On the graph axes shown below, the first two ordered pairs from the table have been plotted. On the same axes plot the remaining pairs.

Write down what you notice.

Recall that each point is plotted by going horizontally first and then vertically.

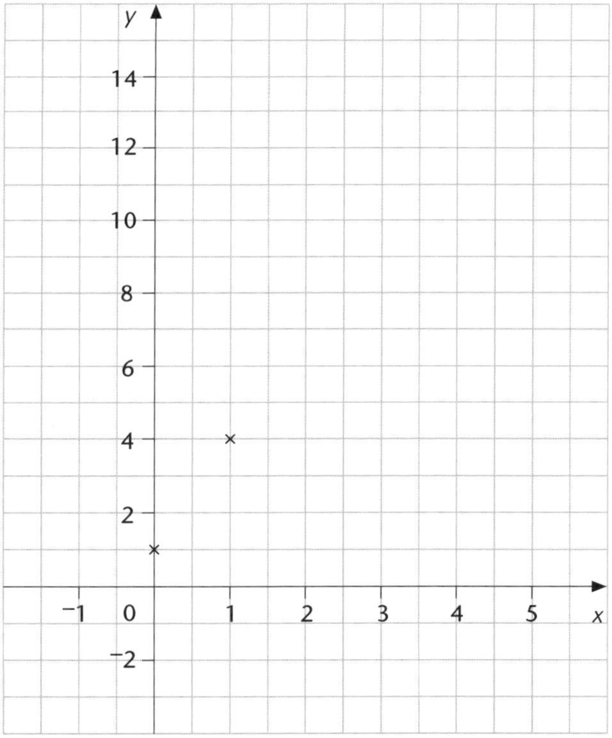

Comment

The points lie in a straight line. This is a way of seeing that there is a pattern or relationship – in this case because the points are in a straight line it is called a **linear** relationship. The next 'higher' point can be generated by moving 1 right and up 3.

If they are not in a straight line, check the plotting of each point. Notice that the scales are different on the x– and y–axes.

Of course, only some of the possible values were chosen for x – the positive whole number values. Since any decimal value or negative value could be chosen, the points on the graph are only a selection. All of the points are represented by the straight line through the plotted points. Draw in the line and extend it to the edges of the diagram.

Plotting graphs

This method of representing a function on a graph allows you to see features that may not be obvious from the formula or table (for example, in the case above, that the points lie on a straight line). This section will examine features of functions that show up on their graphs. The functions studied will all be linear functions, which produce straight line graphs.

To discover the features of linear functions, you need to explore them systematically. The graph plotted above was of the function $y = 3x + 1$. A useful procedure is to vary the numbers in the formula and look at what happens to the graph. Since there are two numbers (3 and 1) it is better to vary only one of them at a time. In the next task the '1' is varied.

Task 25	Drawing lines

If you already feel confident producing tables and plotting points, you may want to use a graphics calculator or computer package to carry out the tasks in the rest of this section.

Create the tables for the functions:

$$y = 3x + 4, \qquad y = 3x - 2, \qquad y = 3x, \qquad y = 3x - 1$$

On the same diagram as you used in Task 24, draw the graphs of these functions.

What do you notice about the lines? Try to generalize your observations.

Comment

The lines are all parallel, but cut the axes at different points. You may have noticed a connection between the numbers that are being varied and the points at which they cut the y-axis. If not, look carefully, and if necessary plot some more functions of the same kind.

The varying number indicates where the graph will cut the y-axis. The technical word for this is the y-**intercept**.

The other number to be varied in the formula $y = 3x + 1$ is the '3'.

Task 26	Drawing more lines

Create the tables for the functions:

$$y = 2x - 1, \qquad y = 5x - 1, \qquad y = x - 1, \qquad y = {}^-2x - 1, \qquad y = {}^-3x - 1$$

Use axes for x from ⁻4 to 4, and y from ⁻5 to 15 to draw the graphs of these functions on a single diagram.

What do you notice about the lines? Try to generalize your observations.

Comment

The lines all pass through the same point on the y-axis ($y = {}^-1$, because they all have $^-1$ as the 'other number'). But they vary in steepness, with two of them sloping down from left to right. You may have noticed that the steeper lines have the bigger numbers, and that the two lines sloping down from left to right have negative numbers. There is a more precise connection between the numbers and the steepness. See if you can find this connection, if necessary plotting some more functions of the same kind.

The steepness of a line is given by its **gradient**. This is found by seeing how much the line rises for a 'run' of 1 across. Notice that you need to take care with the scales here. You must take the actual x and y values – you cannot just count the spaces. The gradient in each of the lines is the number multiplying the x (this is called the **coefficient** of x).

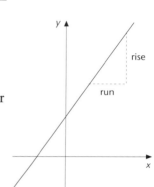

The results of these last two tasks enable you to draw the graph of any linear function without having to create a table. The general form of the linear function is:

$$y = mx + c$$

The value of m gives the gradient of the line, and the value of c gives the point on which it crosses the y-axis.

Identifying lines
Task 27

Identify which lines on the graph below belong with which equation.

$$y = 2x + 3 \qquad y = x + 2 \qquad y = 2x - 3 \qquad y = {}^-3x + 3$$

Comment

A is $y = x + 2$, B is $y = {}^-3x + 3$, C is $y = 2x - 3$ and D is $y = 2x + 3$.

Solving equations with graphs

Being able to plot graphs gives another method for solving equations. Look at the graphs in Task 27. Graphs A and D cross at the point $({}^-1, 1)$. This means that:

$$x = {}^-1, y = 1$$

fit both the equations:

$$y = x + 2 \quad \text{and} \quad y = 2x + 3$$

You can easily check this by substituting the numbers.

Where we have a pair of equations like these, they can be solved by drawing graphs and finding the intersection point. This is an alternative to the algebraic method described on pages 86–88.

Task 28	Solving equations

Use the graphs in Task 27 to solve these pairs of equations.

(a) $y = 2x + 3$ and $y = {}^-3x + 3$

(b) $y = 2x - 3$ and $y = {}^-3x + 3$

Comment

The solution to (a) is $x = 0$, $y = 3$; to (b) it is $x = 1.2$, $y = {}^-0.6$.

The answer to part (b) shows one of the problems of using graphs to solve equations: it is very difficult to get an exact answer. However, if an approximate answer is all that is needed, then plotting graphs can be a useful alternative to using algebraic methods (especially when a graphics calculator or a computer is available).

Task 29	Reflection

Think back over the whole of this section. Try to answer the question 'Where is the algebra?'.

Comment

Your list may include some of the following:

▶ drawing pictures;

▶ counting specialized examples;

▶ predicting the next;

▶ constructing a table;

▶ working out a rule;

- stating the properties of arithmetic;
- expressing rules or relationships in actions, words, and symbols (using expressions, equations, or functions);
- drawing a graph.

In some sense the algebra is in the mathematical thinking – the pictures, words and symbols are records of that thinking. They are a means of communicating your thinking to yourself and, with agreed ways of recording, to other people.

Further reading

Caleb Gattegno (1977) *What We Owe Children*, Routledge and Kegan Paul.

John Mason, Alan Graham, David Pimm and Norman Gower (1985) *Routes to / Roots of Algebra*, The Open University.

Dick Tahta (ed.) (1972) *A Boolean Anthology – Selected Writings of Mary Boole on Mathematical Education*, ATM.

5. Geometry and algebra

Introduction

The origins of the word geometry lie in measuring (*metry*) the earth (*geo*).

Although it is now often called 'shape and space', geometry is the original term for the study of relationships between points, lines, circles, planes and other 2D and 3D objects. Geometry has a very long history, arising from the practical measurement of land in the Nile delta in ancient Egypt and the geometry as developed by the Greeks around 500 BC. Greek geometry did not involve actual measuring, and was the study of properties of shape and space that has developed into the area of mathematics known as geometry today. There are two central aspects to geometry dealt with in this section: relationships and generality.

Practical measurement is dealt with in *Number and measure*.

Lengths, angles, areas and volumes are commonly thought of as involving measurement. But there are many relationships between lengths or areas that do not depend upon measuring. For example, the two diagonals of a rectangle must be equal in length, even though we may not know what this length is; or, if a triangle is equilateral (all three sides are equal), then all three angles must also be equal. Rulers or protractors are not needed to deduce those results. Geometry is about establishing such relationships, usually by thinking and reasoning about diagrams. Of course, the results produced by geometry are often very useful in practical measuring.

See *Number and algebra* for other aspects of generalizing.

Geometry, like all of mathematics, is pervaded by generalizing. What is important is not a specific triangle or a particular circle, but properties of *all* circles, *all* rectangles, *all* triangles. The features of shapes such as lengths, area and volume are frequently expressed in formulas, which use algebra. That is why we have put the two topics 'shape and space' and 'algebra' together here. Algebra is used to express generality when quantities are involved, while geometry is the expression of generality when relationships between points, lines, circles, etc. are involved.

Geometry is an excellent domain for working on developing powers of mental imagery, which will then support both mental mathematics and writing. Consequently, you are often asked to imagine some geometrical objects moving and to visualize the relationships between parts of a figure. You may find this unfamiliar at first, but once you become experienced you will find it a powerful way of relating geometric properties and understanding why various results are true. To capture your imaginings you will often need to draw a diagram as a typical snapshot. There are many drawn diagrams in this section and it is helpful to carry out the reverse process with them: seeing each diagram as a still from some mental film.

If you have access to a computer, you may be able to use a dynamic geometry package which can be very like producing a film on the computer screen that corresponds to your mental one; but, of course, it is much easier to see what is happening.

Often, when referring to parts of a diagram, it is necessary to give them labels. The simplest way might be to colour the lines, so we could speak of 'the red line' or 'the green circle', but that is not possible in this book. Mostly we shall use the age-old device of labelling points *A*, *B*, *C*, … and lines as *AB*, *BC*, … or *a*, *b*, *c*, … and using combinations of them such as 'angle *ABC*'. It is always rather laborious to read, but unfortunately is unavoidable.

Colouring *is* possible with dynamic geometry software.

This section is in four parts:

▸ *basic ideas of shape and space* – points, lines and angles, constructions, and transformations of shapes;

▸ *properties of 2D shapes* – concentrating on quadrilaterals;

▸ *lengths and areas in two dimensions* – length and area relationships for shapes, including Pythagoras' theorem;

▸ *geometry in three dimensions* – some types of 3D shapes and their properties including volumes and areas.

Basic ideas of shape and space

Lines and angles

This section looks at the most basic features of geometry: lines and angles. It considers types of angles, and the properties of angles formed by parallel lines and by triangles.

Types of angles

The diagram shows a fixed arm and a rotating arm (with the arrow), which have an angle formed between them. Imagine the moving arm starting on top of the fixed one and then rotating in the direction of the arrow. Focus on the size of the marked angle. At first the angle is quite sharp, but becoming less so. It becomes a right angle, and then much blunter until the two lines form a straight line. It then starts to 'turn back upon itself' (it is bigger than the other angle formed by the two lines), passes through a three-quarter turn and then, as the arm gets back to the start, lies on top of the fixed arm again. Most of these angles have names:

▸ When the angle is sharp (still less than a right angle) it is called **acute**.

▸ When the arm has rotated through one-quarter of a full turn the angle is called a **right angle**. The two lines are said to be **perpendicular**.

▸ When the angle is between a right angle and a straight line, the angle is called **obtuse** (compare 'thick');

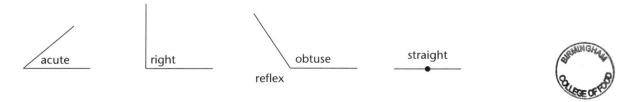

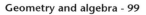

▶ When the angle is greater than a straight line and less than a full turn, it is called **reflex**. (There is no special word for an angle between a three-quarter turn and a full turn.)

Sometimes it is necessary to refer to a turn which involves more than one full revolution, so it is possible to have angles of arbitrarily large size.

Imagine the arm rotating once more, but this time focus on the other angle between the lines. You should see that it behaves in the opposite way to the marked angle: it starts as a reflex angle and decreases. There is a moment when the two lines form a straight line and both angles are equal; then this other angle becomes an obtuse angle, then a right angle, then acute and finally goes to zero.

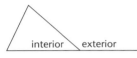

Because there are two angles formed by two lines meeting at a point, we often need to distinguish between them, particularly when referring to angles in shapes. An angle is called **interior** if it is 'inside' the triangle or other polygon. The angle between an edge extended and an adjacent edge is an **exterior** angle.

With the rotating arm, you were able to focus on the marked angle and its 'opposite' angle making a full turn. Instead of thinking of the opposite in a full turn you can also think of opposite angles formed between a pair of lines. In the diagram, the rotating arm now only moves between the two fixed lines. As the arm rotates, the marked angle increases and the opposite angle decreases. When the fixed lines are at right angles the angle and its opposite are called **complementary angles**. When the fixed lines form a straight line the two angles are called **supplementary angles**.

Any pair of angles that make a right angle are called complementary (even when they are not next to each other). Similarly for supplementary.

Task 1	Angles arising from parallel lines

Imagine a straight line on a flat surface. Move it about in your mind so as to get a sense of the freedom you have. Bring it to rest. Make a copy of it and slide that copy around *but* so that it never alters direction, never rotates. Bring it back on top of its original line and hold it still.

Create a third line cutting the first line at an angle (it will also cut the copy). Pay attention to the angles this new line makes with the original line (perhaps even mark one of those angles mentally). Are any of the angles the same size? Again slide the copy. There are now angles between the new line and the copy. How do those angles change as the copy is slid about?

Comment

You should see that the sizes of the angles do not change even though their positions do. There are many equal pairs of angles in the diagram.

When any two straight lines cut, the angles opposite each other are equal (they are called **opposite angles** or, sometimes, 'vertically opposite' angles – although they need not be vertical). This is shown by each pair having the same letter, such as $a = a'$. Because the angles stay the same when the copy is slid about, each of the four angles between the copy and the third line is the same as the corresponding one of the original four angles. Hence the name for such equal pairs – **corresponding angles**.

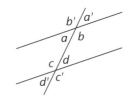

Knowing that opposite angles are equal and corresponding angles are equal, it is quite easy to deduce that other pairs are equal. The equal pair a and d, and the pair c and b are known as **alternate** or **Z-angles** (because they lie in a Z-shape). Perhaps surprisingly, there is no name for the equal pair a' and d' and the pair c' and b'.

Locating equal angles	Task 2

In the margin diagram, lines parallel to the same direction are marked by the same kind of arrows. All the marked angles are equal, either because they are opposite angles or because of the effect of parallel lines. Starting with the heavily marked angle a, you can deduce that any other marked angle is equal to it by following a chain of other equal angles that are each opposite or corresponding or alternate to the previous one. For example, to show that h is equal to a:

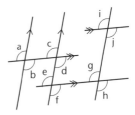

$a = c$ (corresponding) $\rightarrow$ $c = d$ (opposite) $\rightarrow$
$d = f$ (corresponding) $\rightarrow$ $f = h$ (corresponding)

(a) There are other chains that could be made between a and h. Produce two of them.

(b) Find chains between a and j and a chain that takes you back by a different route from j to a.

(c) The diagram below is made up of lines parallel to one of two directions. Mark all the angles you can find which are equal to the marked angle.

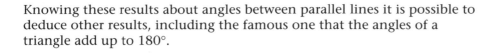

Knowing these results about angles between parallel lines it is possible to deduce other results, including the famous one that the angles of a triangle add up to 180°.

Hint: the two parts of angle d are each equal to one of the angles a and b.

Further comments on the role of proof in mathematics can be found in *Proof and reasoning*.

Angles in a triangle

Look at the figure in the margin. Using the properties of parallel lines it is possible to show that the angle d, an exterior angle of the triangle, is the sum of the angles a and b.

This result is often expressed as:

> The exterior angle of a triangle is equal to the sum of the two interior opposite angles.

This is quite a simple result – but not one that would be obvious just by looking at triangles. It has been produced by reasoning about the properties of angles and parallel lines.

The most famous result about angles in triangles is:

> The sum of the (interior) angles of a triangle is 180°.

What do the different words in this statement contribute? For example, *sum* tells you what operation to perform; *angle* indicates what to attend to; *triangle* provides the context; and 180° tells you what the answer is. But the most easily overlooked word is *a*, because it hides the generality. The statement applies to *every and all* triangles (which lie in a plane). Not just one or two triangles; not just the triangles drawn in a book; but each and every triangle no matter when or where drawn or imagined, or by whom.

Of course, the statement is theoretical: it applies to pure triangles. If you try to measure the angles of a particular triangle then you run into practical problems involving the thickness of lines, the imprecision of a protractor, and so on. Although this result is often given as the 'the angles of a triangle add to 180°', the total angle need not be described as 180° (i.e. in degrees, as if it was being measured). It could be described as 'half a complete turn', 'two right angles', or that the three angles 'fit together to make a straight line'. None of these involve actual measuring.

How do we know that the statement about the sum of the interior angles of a triangle is true? Below are two different proofs: each sheds particular light on the result.

Proof 1

We have shown opposite that the exterior angle of a triangle is the sum of the two interior opposite ones. The third angle of the triangle forms a 'straight angle of 180°' with this exterior angle.

Proof 2

Consider any triangle. Imagine a tiny pencil with the blunt end at a vertex and pointing along one edge of the triangle so that it would traverse the triangle in a clockwise direction. Slide the pencil along the edge until the sharp end is at the next vertex. Rotate the pencil about that vertex corresponding to the interior angle of the triangle until it coincides with the next edge. Repeat the slide and rotation until the pencil is back where it started (but pointing in the opposite direction!). Through what total angle has the pencil rotated? What then is the sum of the angles of the triangle?

Tessellating triangles

Look at the diagram in the margin. Through every vertex of the shaded triangle, a line is drawn parallel to the opposite side. Three more triangles are produced. By the properties of angles and parallel lines it is possible to show that each of these triangles has its three angles the same as the original triangle. In fact, the three triangles are identical (congruent) to the original triangle, but rotated.

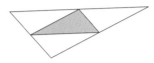

The procedure is repeated by drawing lines through the vertices of the new triangle parallel to each of the opposite sides, and this repeated again, and again, and so on. The whole plane can be covered in this way.

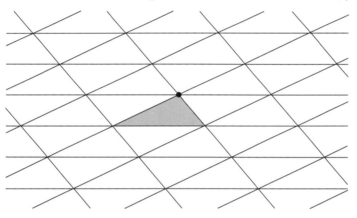

There was nothing special about the triangle used here. All triangles tile the plane.

| Tessellating triangles | Task 3 |

The diagram above shows part of the plane covered in a tiling of triangles.

(a) Look at the diagram in different ways.

- See it as versions of the original triangle. Pick out those triangles that are in the same position as the original triangle.
- See it made up of parallelograms tiling the plane.
- See it as a different set of parallelograms tiling the plane.
- See it as three sets of parallel lines.

(b) Imagine the marked point moving along the horizontal line, dragging the two other sides of the original triangle with it – and, of course, all of the other lines parallel to each of them. Can you make a diagram consisting of rectangles (each with one diagonal)? Can you make the diagram be a different set of rectangles?

This diagram will be used again in the section on transformations.

Comment

The purpose of this task is to assist you in developing your ability to become flexible in your mental imagery and to see shapes embedded in other shapes.

Constructions

There are many constructions used to create different figures but these cannot be dealt with in detail here. This section will give you a way of thinking about constructions that you can use in further work.

Using tools such as rulers, compasses and set-squares to construct geometrical diagrams may seem rather pointless when you can use squared paper, or even a computer. The purpose of thinking about such constructions is not so much to give you methods of drawing (although they do that) as to help you see how shapes can be built up by a sequence of constructions, with each step depending on the previous ones, and to see what are the minimal tools you need for any construction.

Suppose, for example, that you have only an unmarked set-square (a right-angled triangle), so that you can draw a line joining two points and you can draw a line perpendicular to another at any point on it. How could you draw a line parallel to the given line and passing through the point *P*?

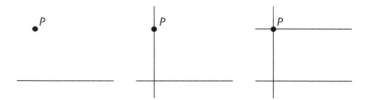

You can do it by using the set-square twice, first to create a perpendicular line through *P* and then another line through *P* perpendicular to that one. This will be parallel to the given line.

You could then draw a rectangle, but you can't draw a square, because you have no way of transferring the length of one side to an adjacent side. For that you need another tool, such as compasses.

| Task 4 | A parallel construction |

A ——————————— *B*

You are given a line segment *AB*. You have use of an unmarked ruler, an unmarked set-square, and compasses. Describe how to draw a square, one of whose edges is *AB*.

Comment

In geometry, **lines** are imagined as carrying on indefinitely in both directions. A **line segment** is a portion of a line.

Use the set-square to draw a line perpendicular to *AB* at *A*. Then use the compasses with centre at *A*, radius *AB*, to draw a circle cutting the perpendicular. That gives three vertices of the square. Now use the set-square to draw a perpendicular at the new point. Use the set-square again to draw the perpendicular at *B*.

To draw a rectangle with given lengths, a similar construction would be used, but with two different sizes of circle.

In fact, once you have compasses, you don't actually need the set-square, because you can use the compasses to do what the set-square does.

Here is a sequence of diagrams to show how compasses are used to draw a perpendicular through the point *P*, as was done with a set-square above. Try to interpret them for yourself before reading the description given.

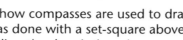

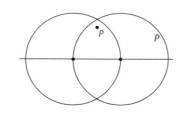

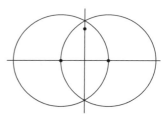

Comment

Draw a circle with its centre at *P*, and cutting the given line in two points. (That circle is now no longer needed.) Draw circles centred at the two new points, and join their two points of intersection. The result is a line perpendicular to the given line through *P*. The reason this works is that all the points on the new line, including *P*, are equi-distant from the two first-constructed points.

This new line is called the **perpendicular bisector** of the two points. It is at right angles to the line joining the points and halfway between them.

2D transformations

Many designs and patterns use transformations of shapes such as rotations and reflections, but transformations are also important because they help make clear connections between shapes and between parts of a shape. To get a feeling for reflections, rotations, enlargements and other transformations, you need to get a sense of what changes and what remains the same.

In mathematics this is often called **invariance**.

Reflecting

There are several practical methods of creating a reflection in a line. Some of them are:

(a) Fold the page along the mirror line and prick the shape through onto the other side.

(b) Copy the shape and mirror line on tracing paper. Turn over the tracing paper and fit the mirror line on top of the original. Press through the shape on the tracing paper onto the page underneath.

(c) Take each point of the original shape and draw a corresponding point the same distance away from the mirror on the opposite side.

In the first diagram below, a polygon is shown reflected in the line. Reflect the other shape in the same line. Reflect the shapes in the second diagram. Was one pair easier to draw than the other? Why?

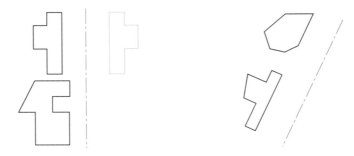

Comment

The significance of this is that to undo a reflection you reflect again in the same mirror line.

The result of a reflection is the shape you see in a mirror placed on the mirror line, viewing from the side the original shape is on. If you view in a mirror from the other side, you should, of course, see an image of the original shape.

People usually find it rather difficult to reflect a shape in a line that is not vertical or horizontal, often making the mistake of having the lines which join corresponding points horizontal rather than at right angles to the mirror line.

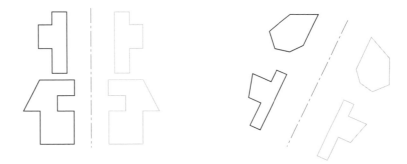

A shape is said to have a **line of symmetry** if that line, when used as a mirror line for a reflection, sends the shape back onto itself.

For each of the shapes shown, sketch in the mirror lines of symmetry.

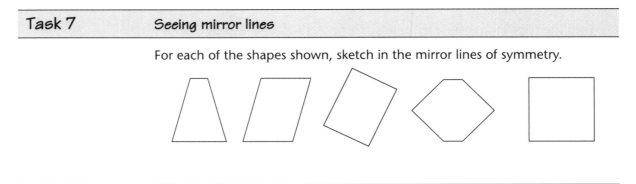

Comment

All of the mirror lines have been drawn in:

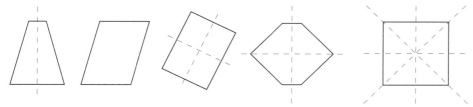

Rotating

Look back to the diagram showing the tessellating triangles (page 103). Pick the shaded triangle and any one of the others that cannot be reached by sliding the shaded triangle. These two triangles are rotations of each other. Put a piece of thin paper on top and make a copy of the original triangle on it. Find a point about which to rotate the top sheet so that the copy lies on top of the second triangle. If the triangle you chose made it easy to find the point (the **centre of rotation**), choose another second triangle that you think might be more difficult. Can you find the centre of rotation for any second triangle? Through what angle does the paper turn?

Every rotation is through a half turn (180°). The rotation points are always, in some sense, 'halfway' between the triangles.

Rotation invariants   Task 8

Use your experience of the rotations of triangles to decide which of the following are unchanged (invariant) by a rotation:

▸ lengths (distances between any two points);

▸ angles (between any two lines of the shape);

▸ the centre of rotation;

▸ a line through the centre of rotation.

What can you say about the distances from the centre of rotation to the top of the shaded triangle and the corresponding point on the rotated triangle?

Comment

Rotation does not change lengths, or angles. The only point which does not move is the centre of rotation. Lines through the centre of rotation will be rotated about that centre.

The distance from the centre of rotation to *any* point of the original triangle is the same as the distance to the corresponding point on the second triangle.

This is useful in doing Task 9.

The centres of rotation for the tessellating triangles were quite easy to find, because all the rotations were through a half turn. When a triangle is rotated about other not-so-special angles, undoing a rotation (finding the centre of rotation) is more complicated.

Suppose triangle *ABC* has been rotated about some point to get to triangle *PQR*. How can that centre of rotation be found, and how many such centres can there be?

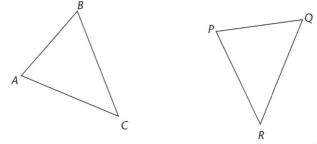

This is a useful place for you to try specializing. Rather than tackle the triangle, first start with some simpler objects.

Take two points (say *A* and *P*), and try to find all points which can serve as a centre of rotation for them. Next, take two corresponding sides of the triangle (say *AB* and *PQ*), and try to find all points which can serve as a centre of rotation for them. Now use these results to help you find the centre of rotation for the triangles.

Comment

The point *A* can be rotated into the point *P* using as centre of rotation *any* point on the line perpendicular to (at right angles to) *AP*, and passing through the mid-point of *AP* (the perpendicular bisector of *AP*). Thus there are infinitely many choices.

To rotate *A* into *P* you must have a centre on the perpendicular bisector of *AP*. Similarly, to rotate *B* into *Q* you must have a centre on the perpendicular bisector of *BQ*. The centre of rotation must lie on each of the perpendicular bisectors, so it must be at their intersection point.

Of course, if *AB* and *PQ* are parallel, there is no such point.

But there is another rotation point because the line segment *AB* could be rotated so that it fits on *PQ* the opposite way, with *A* going to *Q* and *B* to *P*. This second rotation point will be the intersection of the perpendicular bisectors of *AQ* and of *BP*.

There are thus two points O_1 and O_2 which will act as centres for rotating the side *AB* of a triangle to the corresponding side *PQ*. The miraculous thing is, one of those points will be the centre of rotation for *any* triangle with *AB* as a side to rotate to a matching triangle with *PQ* as the corresponding side. The reason is that the rotation does not change distances and angles. So *C*, the third vertex of triangle *ABC*, which is fixed by its distances from *A* and from *B* has to follow and end up in the right place.

Carry out this construction on the triangles *ABC* and *PQR* above.

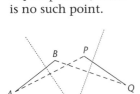

Translating

Look back to the tessellation of triangles on page 103. There are many copies of the original triangle which can be reached simply by sliding the triangle without turning it. These are all **translations** of the triangle. To specify a translation you need to specify a distance to move, and a direction in which to move. In other words, it is only necessary to specify where one point is translated to, for then every point translates by the same amount parallel to that direction.

From the tessellation of triangles pick out the original triangle and one that is translated. How could you convince somebody that it was a translation?

Comment

If you join any point to its translated point, you get a line segment. Joining several points to their corresponding points will give you a collection of parallel line segments all the same length.

Scaling (enlargement)

Scaling (often called **enlargement**) is one of the most important transformations in geometry. It is familiar from photographs being increased or reduced in size and from scale drawings. To scale a figure all lengths are multiplied by a fixed number, the **scale factor**.

Scaly shapes   **Task 11**

Draw your own polygonal shape such as the one shown.

Choose some point on the page, and join it by a line segment to every vertex of your shape, as shown.

Now select a point one-third of the way along each dashed line segment from the chosen point. Join those points up in the same order as their corresponding end points to produce a new shape. What is the same about the two shapes and what is different? What is the scale factor?

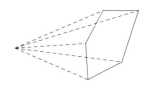

Repeat for a scale factor of one and a half. What if you chose a different fraction or even a negative number?

Comment

Scaling does not change angles. It does change lengths, but all lengths are changed by the same factor. Consequently relationships between lengths are preserved, and that is why the 'shape' stays the same. Two shapes that can be scaled into each other are called **similar**.

Scale factors can be whole numbers, fractions, decimals; they can be larger than one (a true enlargement: making larger) or less than one (making smaller). A scale factor of 1 would leave the shape the same size! Scale factors can also be negative: this means that you go the other side of the centre of the scaling by the corresponding amount.

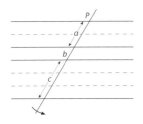

A result about lengths

The ideas of scaling give rise to a result which is quite surprising.

In the diagram, the horizontal lines are equally spaced. Concentrate on the thick lines (the dashed ones are only there to show you how far apart the thick lines are). The thick lines cut the oblique line producing three line segments which have lengths *a*, *b* and *c*. Now imagine the oblique line being pivoted at *P* and swinging in the direction of the arrow. As it swings, the lengths *a*, *b* and *c* change. At first they all decrease until the line is vertical, and then increase again. If the rotating is stopped at any point, what are the connections between the lengths *a*, *b* and *c*? The perhaps surprising answer is that the lengths are always in the same relationship:

$$a = 2b \text{ and } c = 3b$$

This result is attributed to Thales (one of the six 'wise men' of ancient Greece).

Of course, this is only a special case of the result: the spacing of the thick lines can be different from those given, and there can be more than four of them. But the lengths cut off will be always in the same ratios, whatever the position of the swinging line.

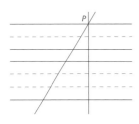

This result is true because it is an instance of scaling. The diagram in the margin shows the line from *P* perpendicular to the thick lines. Each of the four triangles with one vertex at *P* is a scaling of the others: this means that the lengths of the sides, including those on the rotating line, are also scaled versions.

This is the basis for a method in technical drawing for dividing a line into any number of equal parts. (In the diagram the part of the rotating line between the horizontal lines is divided into six equal parts.)

Using coordinates

Coordinate grids are often called Cartesian grids and are named after Descartes (1596–1650).

The method of locating points by coordinates enables geometrical thinking to be assisted by algebra. The standard system of coordinates in geometry requires two axes at right angles with scales the same on both axes. Points are identified by giving the distances from each axis.

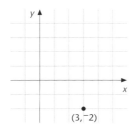

Thus the pair (3, ⁻2) names the point which is found by starting at the origin and travelling three units in the direction of the first axis (the horizontal axis, labelled ***x*-axis**), and then travelling ⁻2 units in the direction of the second axis (the ***y*-axis**).

See *Number and algebra* for more details.

Using coordinates, straight lines and circles can be represented by algebraic equations. An equation such as $y = 2x - 3$ picks out certain points (x, y). For example, it includes (2, 1) and (⁻3, ⁻9). The complete collection of points satisfying the equation gives the geometrical object (in this case a straight line). The coordinates also allow us to look at transformations algebraically.

For more complex transformations you need advanced algebra.

Transforming shapes using coordinates

For simple transformations such as reflection in the *x*-axis, the *y*-axis, or the line $y = x$, and such as rotation about the origin through 90° or through 180°, you can write down the effect of the transformations on coordinates.

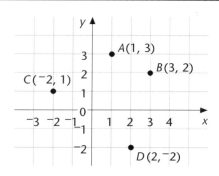

For each of the points A, B, C and D given in the diagram, work out where that point is sent by each transformation.

Transformation	A (1, 3)	B (3, 2)	C (⁻2, 1)	D (2, ⁻2)
Reflection in the x-axis				
Reflection in the y-axis				
Reflection in the line $y = x$				
Rotation about the origin through 180°				

Look along each row, and deduce the effect of each transformation on the coordinates of a point.

Comment

Transformation	A (1, 3)	B (3, 2)	C (⁻2, 1)	D (2, ⁻2)
Reflection in the x-axis	(1, ⁻3)	(3, ⁻2)	(⁻2, ⁻1)	(2, 2)
Reflection in the y-axis	(⁻1, 3)	(⁻3, 2)	(2, 1)	(⁻2, ⁻2)
Reflection in the line $y = x$	(3, 1)	(2, 3)	(1, ⁻2)	(2, ⁻2)
Rotation about the origin through 180°	(⁻1, ⁻3)	(⁻2, ⁻3)	(⁻1, 2)	(⁻2, 2)

To reflect in the x-axis, you change the sign of the x coordinate; to reflect in the y-axis you change the sign of the y coordinate; to reflect in the line $y = x$ you interchange the x and y coordinates; to rotate about the origin through 180° you change the signs of both coordinates.

It is not important that you remember these connections between a transformation and the changes in coordinates. What is important is that you are aware that such connections exist and that you could produce your own examples to find them (or other connections for different transformations).

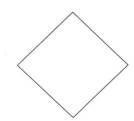

Properties of 2D shapes

Think of the following questions:

▷ What is the name of the shape on the right?

▷ Is a square a rectangle?

▷ What different types of quadrilateral have two lines of symmetry?

These questions indicate the kinds of confusion there can be over naming shapes. The shape here is a square, but might be called a diamond. A square is a particular kind of rectangle, but if you were asked to draw a rectangle you would not normally draw a square. Rectangles and rhombuses have exactly two lines of symmetry, but you could say a square has two lines of symmetry (and also another two – it actually has four). Sometimes shapes are thought of as belonging to a particular class and at other times they are defined as having certain properties.

This section concentrates on quadrilaterals – four-sided shapes – because they are the simplest shapes after triangles and so are most often put into categories and given names. The common types of quadrilateral are shown below:

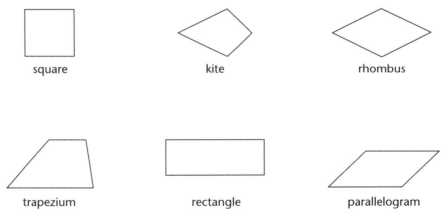

| square | kite | rhombus |

| trapezium | rectangle | parallelogram |

Recognizing shapes

The word 'quadrilateral' may make you think of a parallelogram or a rectangle or some other special type. The aim of the next task is to help you think in terms of the properties that quadrilaterals can have, and to see how these properties can be independent or can be connected.

| Task 13 | Quadrilaterals by properties |

(a) ▷ Draw a quadrilateral.

▷ Draw a quadrilateral with one right angle.

▷ Draw a quadrilateral with two right angles.

▷ Draw a quadrilateral with three right angles.

Now go back and make sure that each example is different.

Now go back and make sure that the example at each stage is *not* an example at the previous stage.

(b) ▷ Draw a quadrilateral.

   ▷ Draw a quadrilateral with one pair of equal sides.

   ▷ Draw a quadrilateral with one pair of adjacent sides equal and one pair of opposite sides equal.

   ▷ Draw a quadrilateral with two pairs of adjacent sides equal and one pair of opposite sides equal.

Now go back and make sure that each example is different.

Now go back and make sure that the example at each stage is *not* an example at the previous stage.

> Take care: 'two pairs of adjacent sides' does not allow three equal sides!

Comment

In part (a) there would be no point in asking you to draw a quadrilateral with four right angles – drawing one with three right angles forces the last one to be a right angle.

Part (b) is trickier. Quadrilaterals with 'two pairs of adjacent sides' are kites. The last set of conditions forces all sides to be equal – the shape must be a rhombus and may even be a square.

A quadrilateral such as a rectangle or a parallelogram has many properties. These properties are interconnected: if a parallelogram has one right angle, then the parallel sides force the other angles to be right angles as well, and so the parallelogram must be a rectangle. The next task looks at this interconnectedness.

Properties of a rectangle	Task 14

Make a list of properties of a rectangle that you know of. Then look at the list in the comment and see which of these you have not included but which *all* rectangles do have. Make a similar list of the properties of a parallelogram.

Comment

A rectangle has four sides – it is a quadrilateral; it has two pairs of opposite edges equal in length and parallel; it has four equal angles; it has four right angles; it has two diagonals which are equal in length; the diagonals bisect each other (i.e. intersect at their mid-points).

A parallelogram is a quadrilateral; it has two pairs of opposite edges equal in length and parallel; it has two pairs of equal angles; it has two pairs of equal sides; it has two diagonals which bisect each other.

Once a quadrilateral has one of these properties, other properties must also be true for that quadrilateral. The initial property can force the shape to have other properties, for example:

The interior angles of *any* quadrilateral add to 360°.

A quadrilateral has four equal angles: that forces the edges to be parallel because of properties of parallel lines, and forces the angles to be 90° since they must add up to 360°. So the quadrilateral must be a rectangle.

A parallelogram has one right angle: that forces it to have four right angles, using properties of parallel lines. So the quadrilateral must be a rectangle.

A parallelogram has equal diagonals: that forces the angles to be right angles (why?). So the quadrilateral must be a rectangle.

A quadrilateral has diagonals which are equal and bisect each other: bisecting diagonals forces it to be a parallelogram and equal diagonals forces it to have right angles. So the quadrilateral must be a rectangle.

Once again, these are not facts to remember. The important thing is to have a sense that because a shape has certain properties, others must also be true, and to be able to deduce them.

Because names and properties get mixed up, disputes can arise about how to classify shapes. Is a square a special kind of rectangle? Is a rectangle a special kind of parallelogram? It really depends whether we define words like rectangle and parallelogram by their shapes or by their properties. The usual practice is to define them by their properties, so any shape which has both pairs of opposite sides parallel is a parallelogram. The next task looks at some special cases.

Task 15	Special cases

Say why the following are true:

(a) A square is a special rectangle.

(b) A rectangle is a special parallelogram.

(c) A parallelogram is a special trapezium.

Comment

The word 'oblong' is often used for rectangles which aren't squares.

(a) Rectangles have opposite sides equal and four right angles. So does a square.

(b) Parallelograms have both pairs of opposite sides parallel. So does a rectangle.

(c) Trapezia have one pair of sides parallel. So does a parallelogram.

Of course, all of the special cases have extra properties which make them special.

Lengths and areas in 2D shapes

Finding lengths and areas for geometrical shapes is not about measuring them. It is about the relationships that there must be between different lengths and areas because the shapes have certain properties. These relationships are usually concerned with different lengths or areas being equal or in some particular ratio to one another. Some have already been mentioned – the connections between lengths on scaled shapes, for example. In this section various results involving lengths and areas are examined. The most famous of these relationships is probably the one known as **Pythagoras' theorem**.

Of course, these properties are often used in practical measuring tasks.

Pythagoras' theorem

Pythagoras' theorem states that the square of the length of the hypotenuse of a right-angled triangle is equal to the sum of the squares of the lengths of the other two sides. Put another way, if you construct squares on the edges of a right-angled triangle, the area of the square on the hypotenuse is the sum of the areas of the squares on the other two sides. Written algebraically, when the three sides are of lengths a, b and c as shown, it is:

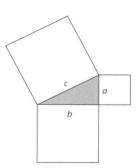

$$a^2 + b^2 = c^2$$

Why is Pythagoras' theorem so important? One reason is that it enables us to calculate distances between points in the plane. Another is that it links areas, lengths, and angles. Egyptian land surveyors used a string with 12 equally spaced knots that could be held as a triangle so that there were 3 units on one side, 4 on the next, and consequently 5 on the next. That gave them a right angle (because $3^2 + 4^2 = 5^2$) to use for marking out property.

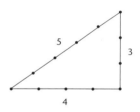

Why is Pythagoras' theorem true?

There are literally hundreds of different proofs of Pythagoras' theorem. Many of them are very algebraic, but others, like the two in the next task, use diagrams.

Two approaches to Pythagoras   Task 16

This task gives two visual proofs of Pythagoras' theorem. You are asked to interpret the diagrams and connect them with the theorem. Each proof works by rearranging the pieces consisting of triangles and squares.

(a)

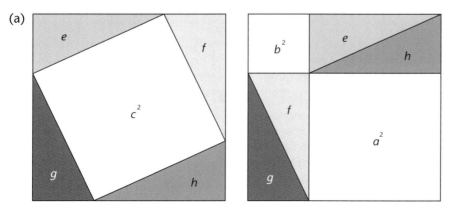

The four identical triangles in the first figure are translated to form the four in the second. Identify which sides of the triangles are *a*, *b* and *c*. Interpret the diagram as a statement about the area of the square on the hypotenuse as the sum of the areas of the squares on the other two sides.

This proof is discussed further in *Proof and reasoning*, page 141.

(b)

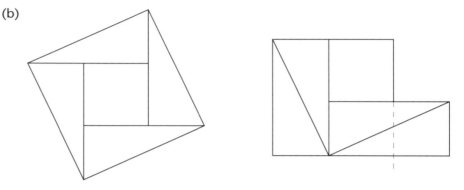

Where is the square on the hypotenuse? Where are the squares on the other two sides?

Think about what aspects of each pair of the diagrams can change, while still remaining a proof of Pythagoras. What is particular and what is general about the diagram (what can change, and what has to stay the same in order to remain 'the same diagram')?

Comment

The triangles have to be right-angled, but the sides can be in any proportions. Note that these approaches to Pythagoras are algebraic in nature, even though based on diagrams.

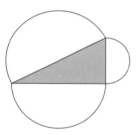

There is a surprising variation on Pythagoras' theorem. Since what matters is the scaling rather than the shape, the theorem applies equally well to other shapes on the edges as long as they are scaled versions of each other. So it also applies to semicircles on the edges.

What is area anyway?

Once you start to think about it, area is a rather elusive notion. It is the amount of space contained within a boundary, which starts out as the number of copies of unit area which would be needed to make up the region.

The area of a rectangle is found by multiplying the lengths of the two sides. This works because it is a way of counting the number of unit squares which will fill a rectangle. So, a rectangle made up of four units in one direction and three in the other has an area of 12 unit squares.

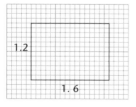

What if the sides of the rectangle were not a whole number of units? If the sides of the rectangle were fractional lengths, then the procedure would be to subdivide the unit squares into sufficiently small squares so that they would pack the rectangle perfectly. For example, a rectangle of sides 1.2 by 1.6 is shown in the margin.

But the area formula applies even when the rectangle cannot be exactly filled by unit squares. For example, if the lengths of the sides are irrational numbers like $\sqrt{3}$ and $\sqrt{5}$ then even though you cannot pack such a rectangle with even the smallest squares, the area is the product of the two lengths. This is another example of how a definition (*area*) is extended from counting numbers so as to include other numbers.

Areas of parallelograms and triangles

The area of a parallelogram is $A = b \times h$, that is, the base multiplied by the height. This is a more surprising result than at first it might appear.

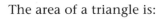

Area of a parallelogram   **Task 17**

Imagine the bottom side of a parallelogram fixed, but the top side sliding along the line. The top and bottom of the parallelogram remain the same length, and the same distance apart, but the other two sides lengthen or shrink. The shape always remains a parallelogram. In one position, the parallelogram will become a rectangle (its sides will be at right angles to the base). Move the top side along again and stop. You should have images something like these:

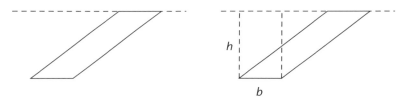

See if you can work out why the area of the parallelogram is the same as that of the rectangle, $b \times h$.

Comment

The area of the parallelogram stays the same and is equal to the area of the rectangle (which of course is $b \times h$). This is easy to see from looking at the diagram in the margin. The rectangle surrounding the whole figure consists of two identical triangles and the parallelogram. Imagine the top triangle sliding to the right: it will fit above the other triangle and leave the rectangle area $b \times h$ to the left, the whole figure is now two triangles and the rectangle. So the area of the parallelogram must be the same as that of the rectangle, $b \times h$.

The area of a triangle is:

$\frac{1}{2} \times \text{base} \times \text{height}$

This is half of the area of a parallelogram with the same base and height. This is easy to see because any triangle is actually half of a parallelogram. It also follows that all triangles with a fixed base and height have the same area.

The area of a trapezium

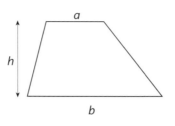

The area of a trapezium is the distance between the parallel lines multiplied by the average (mean) of the lengths of the two parallel sides. It is:

$$\frac{h(a+b)}{2}$$

Task 18	The area of a trapezium

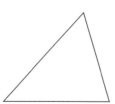

(a) You can use diagrams to show that the formula for the area of a trapezium is true. Each of the first two diagrams can be read to prove the formula. Mark in the lengths a, b and h on each diagram and deduce the formula:

$$\frac{h(a+b)}{2}$$

(b) A special case of the trapezium occurs when one of the parallel edges shrinks to a point. Check that this gives the formula for the area of a triangle.

(c) Another special case of a trapezium is a parallelogram. What extra condition does this put on the lengths of the sides? Check that this can give the formula for the area of a parallelogram.

Comment

The first diagram doubles up the trapezium to make a parallelogram, whose area is $h(a + b)$. Thus the area of the trapezium is half that. The second diagram moves half of the trapezium to make a parallelogram half the height on a base of $a + b$.

When either a or b is 0, the trapezium becomes a triangle and the formula becomes the area formula for a triangle.

A parallelogram is a trapezium with its two parallel sides equal in length. The area formula then gives:

$$\frac{h(a+a)}{2} = ha$$

which is correct for the parallelogram.

Connecting perimeter and area

Perimeter and area measure different things. You can have large area and small perimeter, and relatively small perimeter but large area.

Fixing and changing   **Task 19**

This task involves imagining rectangles, first with a fixed perimeter and then with a fixed area.

(a) A rectangle has a fixed perimeter. Imagine it as tall and thin. Now increase the base until it is long and thin; take it back again. Think what happens to the area.

Consider each of the following statements and decide whether you think it is true (try to justify it) or false (try to find an example which shows it is incorrect).

▶   For any rectangle there is another with the same perimeter but larger area.

▶   For any rectangle there is another with the same perimeter but smaller area.

(b) A rectangle has a fixed area. Imagine it as tall and thin. Now increase the base until it is long and thin; take it back again. Think how the perimeter changes.

Decide whether you think each of the following statements is true or false.

▶   For any rectangle there is another with the same area and larger perimeter.

▶   For any rectangle there is another with the same area and smaller perimeter.

Comment

If you fix the perimeter, then you can make the area get smaller and smaller by making the rectangle longer and thinner. If you try to increase the area, you succeed until the rectangle is a square, and then the area will start to get smaller again as you try to adjust the sides but keep the same perimeter. So the square is a counter-example to the conjecture that the area can *always* be made larger.

If you fix the area, then the perimeter can be decreased until you get to the square, but then can get no smaller. You can make the perimeter get larger and larger by making the rectangle longer and thinner but with the same area. So again the square is a counter-example to the conjecture that you can *always* make the perimeter smaller for a fixed area.

Lengths and areas of circles

If you enlarge a circle of radius 1 by a scale factor of r, then the radius will become r, and the perimeter must be multiplied by r. So the ratio of the circumference to the radius must be constant, independent of the scaling. That ratio turns out to be the number 2π. So the circumference of a circle is given by $C = 2\pi r$.

Area of a circle

Imagine the circle divided into little slices (sectors) and then re-assembled as shown in the diagram.

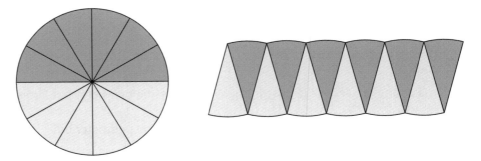

If the sectors are made thinner and thinner, the re-assembly looks more and more like a rectangle. The height of the rectangle will get close to the radius, r, and the length of the rectangle will approach $\dfrac{\text{circumference}}{2}$.

So the area of the circle will be:

For more on such irrational numbers see *Number and measure*.

$$\text{radius} \times \frac{\text{circumference}}{2} = r \times \frac{2\pi r}{2} = \pi r^2$$

The number π expressed in decimals never terminates. It is known to several billion places.

Parts of a circle

The sector of a circle is a slice (like a slice of a round cake).

The area of any sector is a fraction of the area of the whole circle. What fraction? It is easy to see that if the sector were a quarter of a circle, the area would be a quarter of that of the circle, and if the sector were a semicircle, the area would be half that of the circle. In fact, this idea is perfectly general. Whatever fraction the sector angle is of the whole circle, the area will be that fraction of the area of the circle.

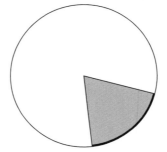

In exactly the same way, the arc length of the sector will be the same fraction of the circumference of the circle as whatever fraction the sector angle is of the whole circle.

Calculations such as these are carried out (usually by a computer) to find the sizes of slices in a pie chart. See *Statistics and measuring*.

Geometry in three dimensions

Although we live in a 3D world, the geometry of three dimensions is more difficult to deal with than that of two dimensions. This is partly because of the difficulty of representing solids by diagrams and descriptions, but it is also because there are more aspects to deal with in three dimensions. In two dimensions, polygons have edges and vertices. In three dimensions, polyhedra have faces, edges, and vertices. In three dimensions, the equivalent of a circle is a sphere. Joining points on a circle needs straight lines, but on the surface of a sphere it involves curves – in fact, circles with differing centres and radii. Again, in three dimensions there are more ways in which shapes can be symmetrical than in two dimensions.

There is no substitute for looking at and handling actual 3D shapes, and so this section can only mention some of the important aspects.

Types of 3D shapes

Even distinguishing between 3D shapes is quite tricky because there are often different ways of seeing the object. Like 2D polygons, there are different ways of classifying them – by a category or by their properties. For example, those made with flat surfaces (the **polyhedra**; singular, polyhedron), or those with, say, four planes of symmetry (e.g. a pyramid). One main category of solids is the **prisms**. These are solids which are 'the same all the way through', and include a cylinder, a Toblerone packet, a shoe box, an unsharpened pencil.

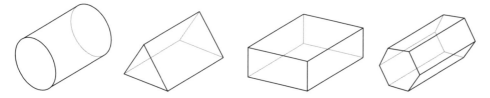

In all these solids, if we cut through them parallel to the end face, we get the same shape as that face. One way of seeing a prism is to imagine the end face translated so that it sweeps out the whole solid.

Recognizing prisms   Task 20

(a) Which of these shapes are prisms?

(b) See a cuboid as a prism swept out from three different 'end faces'.

(c) In how many ways can a Toblerone package be seen as a prism?

(d) In how many ways can a cylinder be seen as a prism?

Comment

The cube and cuboid are prisms, but the cone and pyramid are not. Each pair of opposite faces of a cuboid can be seen as end faces. A Toblerone package is a triangular prism in only one way: the pair of triangular ends serve as end faces. Similarly, a cylinder is a prism in only one way.

Polyhedra

The category of polyhedra overlaps with the prisms: cubes and Toblerone packets are examples of both.

The polyhedra were defined above as the group of solids which have all of their faces made of flat surfaces. A cube and a pyramid are polyhedra, a cylinder and a sphere are not. You probably will have seen examples of the incredibly varied polyhedra that can be produced.

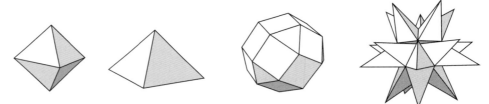

One way of doing so is from **nets** which show the faces to be cut out and folded so as to form the shape. Some examples:

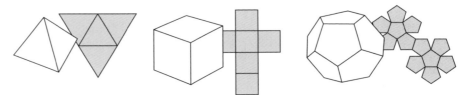

| Task 21 | Netting polyhedra |

Determine what sort of shape the following nets will produce, and decide which lengths have to be equal in order for it to be a net of a polyhedron.

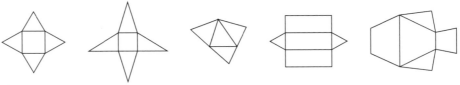

Comment

The first three are pyramids, the fourth is a 'Toblerone prism', the fifth is a wedge.

Properties of solids

There isn't space here to go into details of the properties of 3D shapes, but two can be mentioned: the relationship between faces, edges and vertices on polyhedra, and the symmetries of solids.

Number patterns on polyhedra

Check the following information concerning the number of faces, vertices and edges on three kinds of solids:

Solid	Faces	Vertices	Edges
cube	6	8	12
tetrahedron	4	4	6
pyramid	5	5	8

This surprising relationship was discovered by the German mathematician Euler.

In each case:

faces + vertices = edges + 2

This is true for a wide range of polyhedra (but not for all of them as the following task shows).

| **Faces, vertices and edges** | **Task 22** |

Check whether or not the Euler relationship is true for the following:

Toblerone packet, cylinder, an octahedron, a cube with a square hole cut through it.

Comment

The relationship is true for the Toblerone packet and the octahedron, but not for the cylinder (not a polyhedron) or for the cube with a hole (it is not true in general for solids with holes through them).

Symmetries

As was mentioned above, there are more kinds of symmetry of a solid than of a 2D shape. Here there is only room to mention the most obvious kind: the mirror symmetry in a plane. If you imagine the solid sliced through with a mirror then the two halves must be mirror images of each other. Some examples:

Not all of the mirror planes are shown for each solid.

(a) Find all of the remaining mirror planes for the solids above.

(b) Find all of the mirror planes for these solids:

Toblerone packet, an octahedron, a cube, a cylinder.

Comment

Answers to part (b): the Toblerone packet has 4 mirror planes, the octahedron has 9, a cube has 9 and a cylinder has infinitely many (just as a circle has infinitely many lines of symmetry). These are quite difficult to visualize, even when looking at a model of the solid. It may help to think about the positions of the mirror planes in relation to the edges and vertices of the solids.

Volumes and surface areas of solids

The volumes of cubes and cuboids are found in a manner analogous to finding the areas of squares and rectangles – by multiplying the three dimensions of height, width and depth together. Prisms are slightly more interesting because their volumes are found by multiplying the area of the base by the height. The information on other solids is best conveyed through formulas:

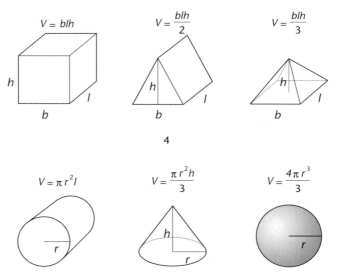

The surface area of a polyhedron is found by adding together the areas of the individual faces.

Look back over the work you have done in this section. As you do so, look for instances where you think:

▎ your knowledge of geometrical relationships has increased;

▎ your ability to visualize geometrical objects has improved;

▎ your awareness of generalizing in geometry has developed.

Further reading

ATM (1982) *Geometrical Images*, Association of Teachers of Mathematics.

Heinz Schumann and David Green (1994) *Discovering Geometry with a Computer*, Chartwell-Bratt.

6. Chance and reasoning

Introduction

This section looks at ways in which the notion of chance is treated in mathematics. The mathematical idea of probability enables us to describe more precisely the likelihood of chance events, especially when there are several such events happening. The section deals with these aspects:

- the use of a probability scale;

- being clear about outcomes from events;

- repeated events and the idea of independence;

- misunderstandings in probability.

Chance and probability

We live in an uncertain world where the unexpected can suddenly strike. Our language is peppered with words and phrases which express doubts, predict expectations or attempt to discuss the likelihood of some event. Here are some of the words and phrases in common use:

very unlikely	possible	fifty-fifty
likely	impossible	an even chance
probable	odds on	certain
quite likely		

Task 1 Sorting chance

Sort the above ten words or phrases in order, from least likely to most likely.

Comment

For most practical purposes when chance events are being described, using words like 'likely', 'very probable', and so on provides sufficient information. However, some of these terms are quite vague and when more precise descriptions of chance events are required, a numerical scale of measure is useful. This is where chance and mathematical probability meet. **Probability** is a way of formalizing chance where the descriptions of uncertainty are measured with numbers rather than described with words or phrases. Probabilities are measured on a scale from 0 to 1, where 0 corresponds to 'impossible' and 1 to 'certain'.

Since there can be no outcome less likely than 'impossible' or more likely than 'certain', probabilities outside the range 0 to 1 cannot occur.

(a) Draw a **probability scale** like the one below. Mark on it your estimate of the numerical probabilities of the ten words and phrases used in Task 1.

```
0                           0.5                          1
├────────────────────────────┼───────────────────────────┤
impossible                                           certain
```

(b) Imagine that a sample of people, chosen at random, were asked to do this exercise. Which words or phrases do you think would result in most and which in least agreement?

Comment

There is no single correct answer to this task but one person's solution is given below.

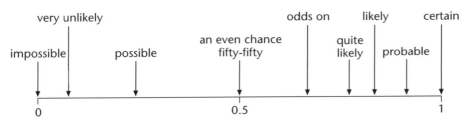

Some terms, such as 'impossible', 'certain' and 'fifty-fifty' (or 'an even chance'), are easy to position as they clearly refer to precise points on the probability scale. 'Likely' will lie somewhere between 0.5 and 1, but where to place it within this range may depend on how optimistic you are. Including 'very' in front of a probability term tends to push its position on the probability scale towards the extremes, whereas using 'quite' pushes its position towards the centre.

'Possible' is a more ambiguous word, as it depends on how you say it. Try wrinkling your nose and say with a dubious tone, 'Well, I suppose it *might* be possible', and you've suggested a low probability. Try it with an enthusiastic smile and say, 'Yes, I really think that *would* be possible', and now you're suggesting a probability between 0.5 and 1.

Outcomes

You may have wondered why textbooks on probability seem to focus on abstract situations like rolling dice, tossing coins and drawing coloured balls out of bags. When asked about the resulting outcomes, one might be forgiven for saying 'Who cares?' You might expect that books would concentrate on everyday events that have chance outcomes – what the weather would be like or whether the bus would be late, and so on. The main reason they don't is related to a fundamental difference between the way in which probabilities are calculated for dice and coins and for everyday events.

The probabilities of the possible events and outcomes associated with dice and coins are clearly defined and can be calculated in advance. By appealing to the symmetries of their shapes we can define the various outcomes precisely and, corresponding to each outcome, allocate a precise probability.

For example, a die is a cube with six faces. Since it is symmetrical, it is a reasonable assumption that each face has an equal chance of landing uppermost, and so the probabilities of rolling a 1, 2, ..., 6 are all the same.

Since it is certain that a throw must give one of 1, 2, 3, 4, 5, or 6, (i.e. a total probability of 1) each of the separate outcomes must have a probability of $\frac{1}{6}$. This is normally written as follows:

$$P(1) = P(2) = P(3) = P(4) = P(5) = P(6) = \tfrac{1}{6}$$

Task 3   Giving a toss

The chance that the coin stands on its edge is so small as to be negligible.

Explain in your own words the following mathematical statement which describes the outcomes of tossing a coin:

$$P(H) = P(T) = \tfrac{1}{2}$$

Comment

This might be expressed as: the probability of tossing 'heads' equals the probability of tossing 'tails' and both are equal to a half.

Probabilities associated with everyday events like the weather cannot be clearly defined and calculated in this way. The best we can do is to keep records over a period of time and count how often the various outcomes occurred. These results can then be used to predict the future. For example, the prospects for an operation might be given as 'There is a 70% chance of it being totally successful'. How is this probability arrived at? It is based on medical statistics: in all the operations of that kind given in the past, 70% have been successful. This appears to be saying that 'If you have this operation, your probability of success is 0.7'. But there is still a further difference from probabilities with dice and coins. The actual operations carried out will not all be identical – they will have differed depending upon the condition of the patient and the ability of the surgeon etc. Additionally, for any individual there may be other factors (unknown to the specialist) which make success more or less likely. Even the meaning of 'success' may be difficult to pin down: there may be side effects or the original condition may recur at a later time.

Dice and coins, on the other hand, are safe and dependable. This makes them a good vehicle for learning about probability and explains why they are so popular in school mathematics. Of course, any die or coin will never be completely symmetrical but it is sufficiently 'perfect' so as to represent a good model for describing and investigating situations of equal likelihood.

Outcomes are often recorded with the aid of **network diagrams** (sometimes called **tree diagrams**). For example, the simple network diagram below sets out clearly the six outcomes that could result from rolling a die. Alongside the network diagram are the associated probabilities of each outcome.

Although these are very simple diagrams, they help to keep the various outcomes clear. As you will see, they are a particularly helpful way of representing outcomes when two or more dice are rolled.

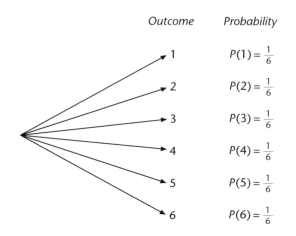

Outcome	Probability
1	$P(1) = \frac{1}{6}$
2	$P(2) = \frac{1}{6}$
3	$P(3) = \frac{1}{6}$
4	$P(4) = \frac{1}{6}$
5	$P(5) = \frac{1}{6}$
6	$P(6) = \frac{1}{6}$

More than one outcome

When outcomes are taken together the result is termed an **event**. More precisely, an event can be either a single outcome or two or more outcomes taken together. Here are two examples of events:

getting a score greater than 4;

getting an even score.

The probability of an event Task 4

Based on a single roll of a die, calculate the probability of each of the following events:

(a) the probability of getting a score greater than 4, $P(\text{score} > 4)$;

(b) the probability of getting an even score, $P(\text{score is even})$;

(c) the probability of getting a score greater than 6, $P(\text{score} > 6)$.

Comment

(a) You may find it helpful to think of the network diagram as branches coming out of a tree. The probability of getting a score greater than 4 is represented by the two branches corresponding to outcomes 5 and 6 and its value is the sum of the separate probabilities of these outcomes.

Expressed in symbols:

$$P(\text{score} > 4) = P(5) + P(6) = \frac{2}{6} = \frac{1}{3}$$

(b) The probability of getting an even score is:

$$P(\text{score is even}) = P(2) + P(4) + P(6) = \tfrac{3}{6} = \tfrac{1}{2}$$

(c) There are no outcomes greater than 6, so this event is impossible. That is:

$$P(\text{score} > 6) = 0$$

The idea can be taken further by considering more complicated events. For example, how would you calculate the probability of getting a score greater than 5 or less than 2? Spend a moment thinking about the use of the word 'or' here. Does it imply *more* branches or *fewer* branches on the network diagram? Does it therefore *increase* or *decrease* the likelihood?

The calculations in Task 5 invite you to put this sort of thinking to work.

Task 5   *More complicated events*

Based on a single roll of a die, calculate the probabilities of the following events:

(a) the probability of getting a score less than 2 or greater than 4, $P(\text{score} < 2 \textit{ or } \text{score} > 4)$;

(b) the probability of getting an even score or an odd score, $P(\text{score is even } \textit{or } \text{odd})$;

(c) the probability of getting an even score or a score less than 3, $P(\text{score is even } \textit{or } \text{score} < 3)$.

Comment

If you concluded that 'or' implies more branches of the tree and therefore is an invitation for you to *add* the probabilities, you were correct!

The solutions are as follows.

(a) $P(\text{score} < 2 \textit{ or } \text{score} > 4) = P(\text{score} < 2) + P(\text{score} > 4) = \tfrac{1}{6} + \tfrac{2}{6} = \tfrac{3}{6} = \tfrac{1}{2}$

(b) $P(\text{score is even } \textit{or } \text{odd}) = P(\text{score is even}) + P(\text{score is odd}) = \tfrac{1}{2} + \tfrac{1}{2} = 1$

> The event in (b) covers all possibilities, and so is a certainty.

(c) A common mistake here is to give the answer $\tfrac{5}{6}$. This is incorrect. The problem is that the two events 'getting an even score' and 'getting a score less than 3' are overlapping; the outcome 'score = 2' occurs in each. So, simply adding the separate probabilities involves double-counting this outcome (which has a probability of $\tfrac{1}{6}$).

The correct answer is found by subtracting the overlapping probability, thus:

$$
\begin{aligned}
&P(\text{score is even } \textit{or } \text{odd}) \\
&= P(\text{score is even}) + P(\text{score} < 3) - P(\text{score is even } \textit{and } < 3) \\
&= \tfrac{3}{6} + \tfrac{2}{6} - \tfrac{1}{6} \\
&= \tfrac{4}{6} = \tfrac{2}{3}
\end{aligned}
$$

Clearly this problem of overlapping events is something of a trap. The simple rule for adding events will only work for events which do not overlap. Such events are known as **mutually exclusive events**. To summarize:

> If two events A and B are mutually exclusive, the probability of A *or* B occurring, $P(A \ or \ B)$, is equal to $P(A) + P(B)$.

> If two events A and B are *not* mutually exclusive, the probability of A *or* B occurring, $P(A \ or \ B)$, is equal to $P(A) + P(B) - P(A \ and \ B)$.

Repeated events

So far you have looked at outcomes and events from a single roll of a die or toss of a coin. Now, think about how you could represent the outcomes and events when a coin or die is tossed twice (two coins are tossed or two dice rolled). Although this might sound complicated, the network diagram keeps it all quite straightforward. For example, when a coin is tossed twice, the four possible outcomes (HH, HT, TH and TT) can be set out clearly as follows:

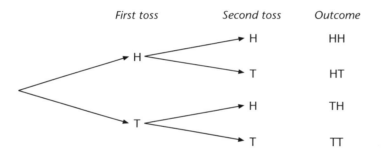

Now the network diagram has two sets of branches. It is helpful to consider them in sequence – first toss and second toss. To return to the 'tree' metaphor used earlier: just as the branches of a natural tree get smaller as they become twigs and then leaves, so too do probabilities as you move from left to right across the network diagram.

Once the outcomes have been set out clearly in this way, you can calculate the probabilities of the various events quite easily. Let us start with the first outcome of HH – i.e. heads on the first toss followed by heads on the second. What is the probability of achieving HH?

This can be understood in common-sense terms as follows:

The probability of achieving heads on the first toss is a half. This fraction further subdivides on the second toss, into a half of a half (i.e. a quarter) in each case. So, $P(HH) = P(HT) = \frac{1}{4}$.

The final column of the following diagram shows how the probabilities are calculated. For example, the probability of tossing heads twice, $P(HH)$, is calculated by multiplying the two separate probabilities together, giving $\frac{1}{4}$.

In the next task you are asked to interpret the information contained in this network diagram.

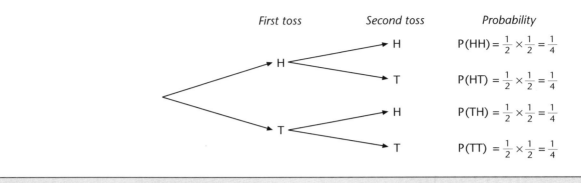

First toss	Second toss	Probability

$P(HH) = \frac{1}{2} \times \frac{1}{2} = \frac{1}{4}$

$P(HT) = \frac{1}{2} \times \frac{1}{2} = \frac{1}{4}$

$P(TH) = \frac{1}{2} \times \frac{1}{2} = \frac{1}{4}$

$P(TT) = \frac{1}{2} \times \frac{1}{2} = \frac{1}{4}$

Task 6	A toss of the head

Using the network diagram above, calculate the probability of:

(a) tossing at least one head;

(b) tossing one head and one tail, in any order;

(c) tossing the same outcome on both coins.

Comment

(a) $P(HH) + P(HT) + P(TH) = \frac{3}{4}$

(b) $P(HT) + P(TH) = \frac{1}{2}$

(c) $P(HH) + P(TT) = \frac{1}{2}$

Independence

Probability is one area where many people's intuition lets them down. The notion of independence is a useful way of describing and debunking some common fallacies.

Task 7	On a roll

A fair coin has been tossed ten times and here are the outcomes:

H T T H T T T T T T

What would you expect the next toss to produce?

Comment

There are several possible responses to this question; here are two incorrect ones:

Incorrect Response A: 'The next outcome is more likely to be heads because there has just been a run of tails.'

Incorrect Response B: 'The next outcome is more likely to be tails because the coin seems to be on a run of tails.'

The correct answer to this question is that the coin is fair and so each toss is independent of what has gone before. Therefore the probability of tossing heads is 0.5 every time the coin is tossed. The reason that people may come up with response A could be to do with some faulty understanding of 'the law of averages'. Although it is true that, in the long run, the proportion of heads settles down to 0.5, it is certainly not the case that a short run of tails will inevitably be immediately compensated by a matching run of heads. The 'settling down' process simply doesn't work like that. The coin has no memory. It does not know that there has just been a run of tails. What happens is that, in a long run, any small irregularities are swamped by the nearly equal numbers of heads and tails. If the coin-tossing continued to a thousand tosses, with equally likely heads and tails, then the eight tails in the first ten tosses would be insignificant.

The mathematical term for this is **independence**. Repeated tossing of coins or dice are independent because the outcome of each new toss is unaffected by the outcomes of previous tosses.

The notion of independence is important when making a formal statement of the rule for multiplying probabilities. On pages 131–132 you saw that the probability of two successive events occurring is found by multiplying the separate probabilities for each event. However, this is true only if the effect of the first event doesn't alter the probability of the second. In other words, the rule assumes that the two events are independent.

Bearing this in mind, the rule for multiplying probabilities can now be stated formally:

> If two events A and B are independent, the probability of A *and* B occurring, $P(A \text{ and } B)$, is equal to $P(A) \times P(B)$.

Common misunderstandings about probability

Here are some of the misunderstandings that many adults have.

The gambler's fallacy

As was discussed in Task 7, it is commonly thought that, when a coin is tossed repeatedly, a recent run of heads is more likely to result in tails at the next toss. This is sometimes called the 'gambler's fallacy', so named because many gamblers believe it and casinos thrive on their foolishness. The fallacy can be exposed by the notion of independence. Random events like rolling dice, buying a winning scratch card or premium bond, choosing a winning set of lottery numbers, and so on, are independent of every other occasion that you do them and carry no memory from one selection to the next.

Equally likely events

A common but mistaken belief is that, if there are only two possible outcomes, they must automatically be equally likely. For example:

> 'I'm taking my driving test tomorrow. I can only either pass or fail, so I must have a fifty-fifty chance.'

Of course, this line of argument is flawed. Dice and coins yield equally likely outcomes but only because of their symmetrical shapes. If you were to toss a drawing pin repeatedly, you will discover that there are only two ways that it can land (on its side and on its back) but these are not equally likely outcomes. Try it and see!

The next task shows another instance of the same fallacy.

Task 8	Equally likely?

Suppose you wish to have a list of the results of 100 tosses of a pair of coins and to save time you use the random number key on your calculator. You ignore any digit larger than 2, and use the digits 0, 1 and 2 to represent, respectively, the outcomes 0, 1 and 2 heads. What do you think the results would look like – and why would they not represent the frequency of tossing two coins?

Comment

You should get roughly equal numbers of each outcome. But the coin-tossing outcomes are *not* equally likely, as you saw on page 132. The event '1 head' is actually twice as likely as the other two (because it can be formed in two ways; HT and TH).

Coincidences sometimes happen

Unlikely events are more common than people tend to believe. Children, in particular, are often too quick to find alternative explanations ('That's more than just coincidence – there must be something out there!') when in fact the phenomenon may simply be one of those occasional glitches that are part of chance variation. For example, in a class of, say, 25 students there is a better than evens chance that at least two of them share the same birthday. For most people this is a surprising result. Two strangers can meet and be amazed to find that they have so many things in common (perhaps they share the same star sign, job and hobby). We should not be surprised by such coincidences. On the contrary, we should be surprised *not* to find them occasionally. If you toss a coin 100 times you will almost certainly get a long run of heads or tails somewhere in your results, just from chance alone. Writing some 2000 years ago, the Greek essayist Plutarch put his finger on the button when he wrote:

> 'It is no great wonder if, in the long process of time, while Fortune takes her course hither and thither, numerous coincidences should spontaneously occur.'

Has your sense of probability been modified in any way by working through this section? To help you reflect, here are some phrases that you have encountered:

mutually exclusive   tree diagrams   adding probabilities
independence   successive outcomes

You may wish to make entries on some of them in your *Mathematical dictionary*.

Further reading

Alan Graham and David Green (1994) *Data Handling, Practical Guide Series*, Scholastic Publications.

Alan Graham (1994) *Teach Yourself Statistics*, Hodder and Stoughton.

The Open University (1990) PM649 *Supporting Primary Mathematics: Probability*, The Open University.

7. Proof and reasoning

Introduction

In this section you are asked to think about reasoning in mathematics. Mathematical reasoning is wider than just proving results. It can involve seeking answers to these questions:

- What is it that is true?

- How can I be sure? What kinds of reasons are convincing?

- Why is it true?

Many of the tasks in other sections of this book have involved you in one or more of these kinds of mathematical reasoning.

What is it that is true? You look for patterns or regularities and start to think a result is true. You then find more evidence for it and become convinced that it must be true; but you may not have any immediate means of justifying your conviction. In other words, you are able to make a **conjecture**.

How can I be sure? Just accumulating evidence is not enough: you have to be certain that there aren't any counter-examples. You need an argument which will prove that the result is true. Often in mathematics, reasoning takes place in logical steps – if such-and-such is true, then *this* follows and then *this*, and so on. This is the activity known as **proof**. It is what you need to convince yourself and, perhaps more clearly stated, to convince other people.

Why is it true? If the argument is correct, a proof establishes the truth of something. But it may not help you see *why* something is true. A not unusual reaction to having something explained logically is 'Well, yes, I can't fault the logic, but I don't see what makes it happen'.

First you are asked to look back over tasks you have done while working on this book and identify places where you carried out some mathematical reasoning.

For example, the lines of shaded circles in Task 1 of Number and algebra.

For example, the proof in Geometry and algebra that angles of a triangle sum to 180°.

Task 1	Recognizing reasoning

Look back through the tasks you have done while working on this book. Find four examples where you were engaged in mathematical reasoning.

Comment

There are many examples you might have picked out depending on which sections you did most work on. Some possibilities are:

Learning and doing, page 6 – following reasoning to show why the sum of the first n odd whole numbers is always equal to n^2.

Number and measure, page 19 – reasoning employed to extend the notion of powers and indices from positive whole numbers to negative numbers.

Statistics and measuring, pages 69–70 – reasoning used to explain why some graphs can be misleading.

Number and algebra, pages 86–88 – reasoning involved in comparing pairs of equations to get a solution.

Geometry and algebra, pages 107–108 – reasoning to deduce how to find a centre of rotation for two triangles.

Chance and reasoning, page 131 – reasoning used to determine how many outcomes are possible when two coins are tossed.

In some of the cases cited above reasoning is used to understand a situation better, in others to make sure that a general result is true in all possible cases. Mathematical proof has similar roles. Mathematicians prove results in order to establish them irrefutably as part of what is known in mathematics, but they are pleased when they prove them in ways that show how these results relate to other known results, hence organizing and clarifying whole areas of mathematics.

Although proving very abstract and specialized results is hard work, proof can be used to clarify and establish quite accessible ideas. This section attempts:

▶ to help you become more aware of kinds of mathematical reasoning;

▶ to make clearer several different types of mathematical reasoning;

▶ to help you read proofs you may come across in mathematics texts.

What is true?

Before there can be any proof there must be something to be proved. In the next task there is no claim, just a problem. You are asked to specialize and then make a conjecture, which can be proved or disproved later in this section.

Deciding what   **Task 2**

Take any two numbers that sum to one.

Square the larger and add the smaller.

Square the smaller and add the larger.

Which result will be bigger?

Conjecture and then think about how you would convince someone else of the truth of your conjecture.

Notice that 'numbers' here cannot just mean whole numbers as there would be hardly any cases to consider.

$\frac{1}{4} + ? = 1$

$0.7 + ? = 1$

$^-3 + ? = 1$

Comment

How many cases did you try before you formed your conjecture? Did more cases make you more sure?

Did you try fractions or decimals or positive and negative numbers or a mixture of these? Did you use algebra to express what you saw, perhaps using a and b to stand for the two numbers? What if either of a or b is zero?

On page 147 of this section a proof will be given of a result which you might have conjectured.

Sometimes in mathematics, reasoning is used to decide not just *whether* something is true, but rather *when* it is true. Bear this in mind when you try the next task.

Task 3	Deciding when

Look at these three algebraic statements:

$$2x > x + 2$$

$$2x = x + 2$$

$$2x < x + 2$$

They seem to contradict each other. Does that mean they are all untrue? Or that some of them are untrue? Or might they all be true some of the time? What do you think and why? Specialize to particular values of x: try to find when each statement is true.

Comment

Perhaps the middle one is the easiest to think about. Is it possible that $2x = x + 2$?

Well, yes it is, because by treating the statement as an equation to be solved you find that $x = 2$. So a true statement is that:

$$2x = x + 2 \text{ when } x = 2$$

Specialize? For example when $x = 3$, then $2x = 6$ and $x + 2 = 5$.

What happens when x is more or less than 2?

In fact, if $x > 2$, adding x to both sides of the inequality gives $x + x > 2 + x$. Therefore:

$$2x > x + 2 \text{ when } x > 2$$

For example, when $x = {}^-3$, then $2x = {}^-6$ and $x + 2 = {}^-1$.

Similarly, if $x < 2$, adding x to both sides of the inequality gives $x + x < 2 + x$.

$$\therefore \quad 2x < x + 2 \text{ when } x < 2$$

The above comment has several features which are often used when something is proved in mathematics.

▷ All possible cases are considered. In this context x must be greater than 2 *or* equal to 2 *or* less than 2. There are no other possibilities.

Mathematicians like to do as little work as possible, so they look for arguments which will work in several situations. They are also fond of succinct symbols.

▷ The third case starts with the word 'Similarly'. The word 'similarly' is used to indicate that the logical structure of the argument here is the same as in the previous case.

▷ The last line in the third case starts with the symbol '$\therefore$'. This is simply a mathematical abbreviation for the word 'therefore', indicating that the result follows from the previous statement.

This example is a good illustration of how you can by logical reasoning prove something but gain little insight into why it is true. It tells you exactly which is the greater of $2x$ and $x + 2$, but offers no reason why. The proof does not make it clear, for example, whether the reason $x = 2$ is a crucial value is connected to the 2 in $2x$, or the 2 in $x + 2$, or neither. Visualizing the example may give you more insight. If you draw the graphs of $y = 2x$ and $y = x + 2$ on the same axes, it shows you clearly which is the greater and when.

Drawing a graph is also useful because if you change some of the values and have, say, $x + 3$ instead of $x + 2$, it is easy to see what the effect would be.

A note on notation

The most familiar of the many symbols which are used in mathematics are probably the numerals 0, 1, 2, 3, 4, 5, 6, 7, 8 and 9 together with the decimal point '.' and the operation signs +, -, × and ÷ which make it possible to write down calculations.

One very common symbol which deserves special mention is the equals sign '=' which was invented by Robert Recorde who wrote in *The Whetstone of Witte* (1557) that he had chosen this form 'bicause noe 2 thynges can be moare equalle'. It may seem obvious to say that it is used to show that two things are equal as in:

$2 \times 5 = 10$ or $2x = x + 2$

but it is all too often misused when a sequence of calculations is performed. For example, look at the following version of a calculation:

$7 + 5 = 12 \times 75$
$\qquad = 900 + 8 + 9 = 917$

While you might understand what was intended, as written this is nonsense since 12×75 is not equal to either of $7 + 5$ or $900 + 8 + 9$, as is apparently claimed. What is meant is:

$7 + 5 = 12$
$12 \times 75 = 900$
$900 + 8 + 9 = 917$

with each intermediate answer being used as part of the next calculation.

Notice how this written version contrasts with key presses when using a calculator to carry out the calculations. On an ordinary four-function calculator you would press:

7 $\boxed{+}$ 5 $\boxed{\times}$ 75 $\boxed{+}$ 8 $\boxed{+}$ 9 $\boxed{=}$

As was seen in Task 3, '=' can be used when the statement is only sometimes true. Whenever you see an equation to be solved, you can read it as 'For what values of the unknown(s) is this statement true?'

Sometimes it is important to emphasize that a statement is always true. For this purpose the symbol '≡' is used. So, for example, you may see the statements which were written in *Number and algebra* (page 80) as:

$a + b = b + a$ and $a \times b = b \times a$

You may find it helpful to include some entries on symbols and notation in your *Mathematical dictionary*.

Pressing another operation key automatically performs the previous operation.

written as:

$$a + b \equiv b + a \qquad \text{and} \qquad a \times b \equiv b \times a$$

to indicate that they are true for all possible values of a and b.

One way of becoming confident in your use of notation is to read mathematical statements aloud.

The first of these, $a + b \equiv b + a$, is read aloud as 'a plus b is *always* equal to b plus a'. Try reading the second one, $a \times b \equiv b \times a$, aloud.

Another symbol which looks rather like an equals sign but which has a quite different purpose is the *implication* symbol which is written '$\Rightarrow$' as in:

$$x < 2 \Rightarrow 2x < x + 2$$

This statement is read aloud as 'x is less than 2 *implies that* $2x$ is less than x plus 2' or as '*if* x is less than 2, *then* $2x$ is less than x plus 2'.

The process of proving

In the next two tasks we use the symbols $\equiv$, $\Rightarrow$ and $\therefore$ when appropriate.

This section examines what is needed to prove a result in mathematics, and some particular kinds of proof.

Making reasoning more precise

In many places in this pack there has been informal reasoning to show that a result is true. While these arguments are often immediately convincing, a critical person could point to assumptions that have not been proved, or cases that have been ignored. In this section two proofs are looked at more closely.

Task 4	Always true

A common mistake in algebra is to write $(a + b)^2 = a^2 + b^2$.

Look at the statement below:

$$(a + b)^2 \equiv a^2 + 2ab + b^2$$

Convince yourself that it is true – perhaps by specializing, perhaps by visualizing the area of a square of side length $a + b$.

Think about how you might convince someone else that it is true.

Comment

An informal 'proof' is shown in the diagram in the margin. Diagrams like this were given in *Number and algebra* (page 82) as a visualization of the properties of numbers. Although they help to make clear the 'rules' of algebra, they only really make sense when a and b are positive numbers. The properties of numbers such as the commutative and distributive ones can be used to give a precise way of proving the statement as follows.

	a	b
a	a^2	ab
b	ba	b^2

By using the distributive property twice:

$$(a + b)^2 \equiv (a + b)(a + b) \equiv (a + b)a + (a + b)b$$
$$\equiv a^2 + ab + ba + b^2$$

Because multiplication is commutative:

$$ab \equiv ba$$

$$\therefore \quad ab + ba \equiv ab + ab \equiv 2ab$$

$$\therefore \quad (a + b)^2 \equiv a^2 + 2ab + b^2$$

This argument would be equally valid if '=' had been used rather than '≡'. However, '≡' emphasizes that each step is true for all values of a and b.

Sometimes results which look like algebra are really about particular lengths rather than about numbers in general. For example, Pythagoras' theorem, which is often written down in the form:

$$a^2 + b^2 = c^2$$

is about those sets of lengths which can form the sides of a right-angled triangle. Here diagrams capture much more of the generality. Look at the two diagrams below.

Here it would be wrong to use ≡ since it is not always true – only for certain a, b, c.

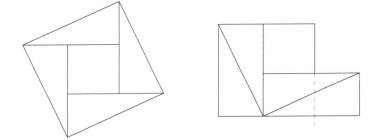

These are copies of the diagrams on page 116 of *Geometry and algebra*.

Each shows four copies of a right-angled triangle together with a small square. In the first diagram the five pieces are arranged inside a square whose side is equal to the length of the hypotenuse of the triangle; in the second they are re-arranged to make two squares. This claims to prove Pythagoras' theorem. A sceptical person might ask: 'How do the diagrams prove Pythagoras' theorem, and how do you know those are squares?'

To help explain this it is useful to assign the letters to the lengths of sides of the four identical triangles. In what follows:

    c = the length of the hypotenuse (i.e. the side opposite to the right angle);
    a = the length of the shortest side of the triangle;
    b = the length of the remaining side of the triangle.

Proving Pythagoras   Task 5

Read the following proof of Pythagoras' theorem carefully. First, try to get a sense of the whole argument, and then look carefully at each step and work out what is being claimed.

Stage 1. What do the diagrams show?

    Both diagrams are made of exactly the same pieces (four identical triangles and a small square), so they must have the same areas. The left-hand diagram is a square whose side is c. So its area is c^2. The right-hand diagram, made of the same five pieces, appears to be two squares (shown by the dashed line). One is the square on the shortest side (and so of area a^2), the other is the square on the third side (of area b^2).

Because the area of the five pieces was previously c^2 and is now $a^2 + b^2$, this proves Pythagoras' theorem, $a^2 + b^2 = c^2$. But are the parts of each diagram actually squares? How can we be sure?

Stage 2a. Proving that the left-hand diagram is a square:

To be squares, shapes must have all sides equal and their interior angles must be right angles.

In the left-hand diagram, the sides of the 'square' are all equal because they are all the longest side of the triangle. Are the angles right angles? Each is made up of two of the angles of the triangle. Since the third angle of the triangle is a right angle and the angles of any triangle add to 180°, then those two angles must add to 90°. So it is a square.

Stage 2b. Proving that the right-hand diagram is two squares:

Both parts do have right angles at their corners (and so must be at least rectangles), but we need to show that the sides are all b for the larger 'square' and a for the smaller. In fact, it is easy to work out the lengths using simple algebra.

On each of the diagrams, mark the lengths of the sides a, b and c. From the left-hand diagram, show that the length of each side of the little central square is $b - a$.

Now mark these lengths of the sides of the small square on the second diagram.

The top edge of the big 'square' is now $a + (b - a) = b$. Thus it is a square, with all sides of length b.

Similarly, work out the length of the top side of the small 'square'. It is the overall length, $a + b$, less the side of the large square, b. That is, $a + b - b = a$. So this part is also a square.

Stage 3.

The result is now proved: the parts in each diagram are squares of sides c (in the left-hand diagram) and a and b (in the right-hand diagram) and are equal in area.

Deductive proofs

Proofs that involve logical chains of reasoning, starting with what is known and going step by step to a conclusion, are known as **deductive proofs**. This section discusses some examples of such proofs.

Task 6	Does it follow?

In this task 'number' means 'whole number' since the phrase 'is divisible by' only applies to whole numbers.

Think about whether or not the following statements are true, then try to prove (or disprove) them.

(a) If a number is divisible by 6, then it is divisible by 3.

(b) If a number is divisible by 7, then it is divisible by 14.

Comment

(a) This is true. If a number is divisible by 6 then it can be partitioned into six equal parts. Imagine joining those six parts together in pairs; the result will be three equal parts, which is the same as saying the original number is divisible by 3.

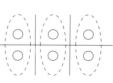

To express this more formally, call the original number n and each of the six equal parts k. Expressed algebraically this gives:

$$n = 6 \times k = 6k$$

But $6 = 3 \times 2$ so:

$$n = 3 \times 2 \times k$$

In other words:

$$n = 3 \times 2k = 3(2k)$$

That is, n is divisible by 3.

(b) This time the statement is not true in general. To disprove it we need only to produce one case (a counter-example) where it does not work.

So, for example, we can simply say that the number 21 is divisible by 7 (in fact it is equal to 7×3) but it is not divisible by 14.

Note that even though (b) is not true in general, it is often true for particular values. For example, the number 28 is divisible by 7 and is also divisible by 14.

The true statement in (a) above could be written using the implication symbol, as:

n is divisible by $6 \Rightarrow n$ is divisible by 3

Notice that implication does not necessarily work both ways round. In this case the **converse** statement:

n is divisible by $3 \Rightarrow n$ is divisible by 6

is not a true statement (using a similar argument to that in part (b) of the comment).

In the next task two statements are given, together with their converses.

Arguing conversely   Task 7

Look at the two pairs of statements. Decide whether each statement in each pair is true or not. Prove each true statement using a deductive argument, and disprove each false statement by producing a counter-example.

Statement A: If m and n are both even numbers, then $m + n$ is an even number.
Converse A: If $m + n$ is an even number, then m and n are both even numbers.

Statement B: If n is an even number, then n^2 is an even number.
Converse B: If n^2 is an even number, then n is an even number.

Comment

Three of the statements are true. The exception is converse A, for which you might have found many counter-examples, for example taking $m = 3$ and $n = 5$.

For the second pair both B and its converse are true, that is:

$$n \text{ even} \Rightarrow n^2 \text{ even} \quad \text{and} \quad n^2 \text{ even} \Rightarrow n \text{ even}$$

The two statements can be combined symbolically by writing:

$$n \text{ even} \Leftrightarrow n^2 \text{ even}$$

which is read as:

'*n* is even *if and only if* *n*-squared is even.'

You probably found converse B hardest to prove since you need to bring in some information that is not explicitly stated, namely that the square of an odd number is always odd. In a situation like this it can help to prepare for proving by organizing ideas into what you know and what you want.

In this case:

I know that	*n*-squared is even.
I want to show that	*n* must be even.
I also know that (How do I know?)	the square of an odd number is odd.

So a deductive proof of converse B might go something like this:

It is shown in *Learning and doing* (page 6) that the *n*th odd number can be expressed as $2n - 1$, so the *k*th odd number is $2k - 1$. For example, if $k = 10$ then $2k - 1 = 19$.

Any odd number can be written in the form $2k - 1$, where *k* is a whole number.

So the square of an odd number is of the form $(2k - 1)^2$.

$(2k - 1)^2 = 4k^2 - 4k + 1 = 2(2k^2 - 2k + 1) - 1$ which is odd. (Recall Task 4.)

So if *n*-squared is even then *n* cannot be odd.

∴ *n* is even.

Although algebra can be a very useful way of expressing generality it does not follow that all deductive proofs are algebraic. For example, two proofs that the angle sum of a triangle is 180° were indicated in *Geometry and algebra*.

The first of these outlined a traditional proof. The next task is to make sense of a more formally presented deductive version of this proof.

Task 8   Take any triangle

This proof is in a style which many textbooks use. It sets out a deductive argument in a formal language. You will need to work through the proof line by line, but also try to get a sense of the whole. At the end you might find it useful to compare it with the version given in *Geometry and algebra* (page 102), and think about the different notations and methods of setting out the proof.

Theorem: The sum of the angles of a triangle is equal to 180°.

Consider the triangle *ABC* shown in the diagram.

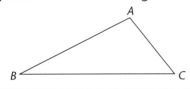

Construct a line *PQ* through *A* parallel to *BC*.

∠ *PAB* = ∠ *ABC* (since they are corresponding angles)

∠ *QAC* = ∠ *ACB* (since they are corresponding angles)

So   ∠ *ABC* + ∠ *BAC* + ∠ *ACB* = ∠ *PAB* + − *BAC* + ∠ *QAC*

But   ∠ *PAB* + ∠ *BAC* + ∠ *QAC* = 180° (since they form a straight line)

∴   ∠ *ABC* + ∠ *BAC* + ∠ *ACB* = 180° as required.

Proof by exhaustion

There is another useful method of proof which is very simple to understand. It is used when there is only a small number of cases to consider, and each one can be checked. This type of proof is called **proof by exhaustion**. Two examples, one from probability and one from geometry, show how the method can be used.

'Proof by exhaustion' because you exhaust (use up) all of the possibilities.

Throwing two dice

Two dice, one red and one blue, are rolled and the numbers on their uppermost faces are added.

The claim here is that there are eleven possible totals and the total 7 occurs most frequently among the possible outcomes.

Proof: The red die is represented by R and the blue die by B. The table lists all possible combinations of scores on the two dice.

R/B	1	2	3	4	5	6
1	1 + 1 = 2	1 + 2 = 3	1 + 3 = 4	1 + 4 = 5	1 + 5 = 6	1 + 6 = 7
2	2 + 1 = 3	2 + 2 = 4	2 + 3 = 5	2 + 4 = 6	2 + 5 = 7	2 + 6 = 8
3	3 + 1 = 4	3 + 2 = 5	3 + 3 = 6	3 + 4 = 7	3 + 5 = 8	3 + 6 = 9
4	4 + 1 = 5	4 + 2 = 6	4 + 3 = 7	4 + 4 = 8	4 + 5 = 9	4 + 6 = 10
5	5 + 1 = 6	5 + 2 = 7	5 + 3 = 8	5 + 4 = 9	5 + 5 = 10	5 + 6 = 11
6	6 + 1 = 7	6 + 2 = 8	6 + 3 = 9	6 + 4 = 10	6 + 5 = 11	6 + 6 = 12

By examining the results you can see that there are eleven possible totals (namely 2, 3, 4, 5, 6, 7, 8, 9, 10, 11 and 12).

Moreover, the total 7 occurs in six different outcomes which is more than any other total (in fact 2 and 12 occur once each, 3 and 11 occur twice, 4 and 10 three times, 5 and 9 four times and 6 and 8 five times each.)

Fitting squares

A domino is formed by joining two equal squares edge to edge.

A tromino is formed by joining three squares, so that each square is joined edge to edge with its neighbour.

The claim here is that there are exactly two possible trominoes.

If two shapes are identical then one can be fitted exactly on top of the other by a combination of translating, rotating and reflecting.

Proof: Start with a domino and add one square to each of the free edges in turn as in the diagram. This generates all possible cases.

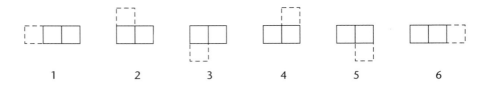

| 1 | 2 | 3 | 4 | 5 | 6 |

Cases 1 and 6 are identical.

Similarly, cases 2, 3, 4 and 5 are identical.

There are therefore exactly two distinct trominoes.

Task 9	Exhausting possibilities

A tetromino is formed by joining four squares, so that each square is joined edge to edge with its neighbour.

Prove that there are exactly five tetronimoes.

Proving conjectures

Finally, we return to two tasks which were left unfinished: Task 2 from this section and a task that was left as a challenge on page 8 of *Learning and doing*.

Task 10	Return to one sum

Look at your notes for Task 2. See if you can use any of the ideas you have met in this section to clarify the thoughts you had then.

Next, read through the comment below and then the text that follows it. You should try to get a sense of the whole proof and also see what each step contributes.

Comment

When you attempted the problem you should have found that for each pair of numbers *a, b* that you chose, then:

$$a^2 + b = a + b^2$$

and the more numbers you tried, the more convinced you were likely to be. However it is clearly impossible to attempt a proof by exhaustion. A deductive proof is shown below.

The formal proof is set out with informal thinking and comments side-by-side.

Informal thinking	Theorem

Informal thinking

I want to show that $a^2 + b = a + b^2$.

The plan: I can't assume that $a^2 + b = a + b^2$, so I will take each side of it separately and show they are the same.

I know that $a + b = 1$, so I can write $b = 1 - a$. By substituting for b, I can express both sides of the equation in terms of a.

I put $b = 1 - a$ into the left-hand side and simplify it using algebra.

I put $b = 1 - a$ into the right-hand side and simplify it using algebra.

Both sides are the same, $a^2 - a + 1$.

Theorem

$$a + b = 1 \Rightarrow a^2 + b = a + b^2$$

Proof

$$a + b = 1 \Rightarrow b = 1 - a$$

so for any pair of numbers a and b which sum to 1:

$$a^2 + b = a^2 + (1 - a) = a^2 - a + 1$$

and:

$$a + b^2 = a + (1 - a)^2 = a + 1 - 2a + a^2$$
$$= a^2 - a + 1$$

It follows that:

$$a^2 + b = a + b^2$$

and hence the conjecture is proved.

Here is one more result to be proved.

Sum challenge   **Task 11**

The following statement was left as a challenge on page 8 of *Learning and doing*.

> The sum of the first n numbers is equal to half of the sum of n^2 and n.

Look back at any notes you have already made about this claim and see if you can expand or clarify them.

Comment

Read through the discussion below. Again, try to follow the argument as a whole and also work out why each step is there. Does the train of thought correspond to your own or did you take another route? Perhaps you noted other aspects from those mentioned.

First the claim is written more succinctly using algebra. The nth counting number is n so the statement is now written as:

$$1 + 2 + 3 + \cdots + (n-1) + n = \tfrac{1}{2}(n^2 + n) = \tfrac{1}{2}n(n+1)$$

$1 + 2 + 3 + \cdots + (n-1)$ can be visualized as a growing triangle:

The numbers formed are in fact known as the triangle numbers.

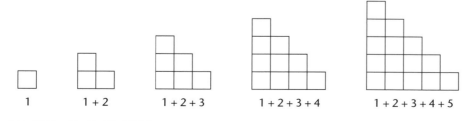

| 1 | 1 + 2 | 1 + 2 + 3 | 1 + 2 + 3 + 4 | 1 + 2 + 3 + 4 + 5 |

Try comparing the result with the formula for the area of a triangle. (See *Geometry and algebra*, page 117.)

and if two copies of, say, the 5th triangle are put together a 6×5 rectangle is obtained:

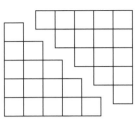

which shows that the fifth sum is equal to half of 6×5.

It is possible to 'see' that the same process can be used for any of the triangle numbers – but not to draw the nth case. Once more algebra can be called upon to deal with the general case.

Let s = the sum of the first n counting numbers. Then:

$$s = 1 + 2 + 3 + \ldots + (n - 1) + n$$

Reversing this gives:

$$s = n + (n - 1) + (n - 2) + \ldots + 2 + 1$$

Viewing the two versions together reveals n pairs of numbers with each pair adding to $n + 1$. So:

$$2s = n \times (n + 1)$$

From which:

$$s = \tfrac{1}{2}(n \times (n + 1)) = \tfrac{1}{2}(n^2 + n)$$

as required.

Task 12   *Reflect and connect*

Look back over your work on *Proof and reasoning*. Make brief notes on any new things you have learned or new connections you have made, updating your *Mathematical dictionary* as necessary.

Further reading

Leone Burton (1994) *Thinking Things Through*, Blackwell.

John Mason, Leone Burton and Kaye Stacey (1996) *Thinking Mathematically*, Addison-Wesley.

8. Practice exercises

Introduction

This section provides sets of exercises for you to practise rules and techniques of which you are unsure. Here is some guidance for using this section.

▶ The aspects of mathematical thinking described in *Learning and doing* are relevant when you work on these. Using 'I know', 'I want' and 'I have' will often help when you are stuck.

▶ You should not necessarily do all the exercises in a group – once you have achieved reasonable fluency it is not a good use of your study time to practise further.

▶ Conversely, you may feel that you would like more exercises than are given for a particular topic. One way of deepening your understanding of that topic is to make up similar questions of your own. First try to produce a simple example of that type, then a harder one, and then see if you can answer your own questions.

▶ Following on from producing your own questions, you could then try to write down what you see as the generality of which the questions in that set are particular cases.

The solutions start on page 156.

Exercises

Number and measure	Exercises
(a) Express each of the following percentages as fractions:	NM.1

    (i) 40%   (ii) 8%   (iii) 70%   (iv) 67%

(b) Express each of the following percentages as decimals:

    (i) 50%   (ii) 85%   (iii) 7%   (iv) 16%

(c) Convert each of the following to percentages:

    (i) 0.8   (ii) 0.21   (iii) 2.4

    (iv) $\frac{1}{2}$ (v) $\frac{1}{8}$ (vi) $\frac{1}{9}$

A survey was carried out on 840 married couples to investigate family income. 75% of the wives were in paid employment; 40% of the husbands had annual salaries over £18 000; 18% of the couples had a joint income of less than £120 per week.

NM.2

(a) How many wives were in paid employment?

(b) How many husbands earned over £18 000 per year?

(c) How many couples had a joint income of less than £120 per week?

NM.3   Express each of the following numbers in standard form.

     (a) Light travels 9 460 700 000 000 km in a year.

     (b) The distance from the centre of the Earth to the centre of the Moon is 384 400 km.

     (c) Saturn is 1 427 000 000 km from the Sun.

     (d) The mass of the Earth is 5 976 000 000 000 000 000 000 000 kg.

     (e) The Mediterranean Sea has an area of 2 504 000 km^2.

     (f) Annapurna I is 8091 m high.

NM.4   Express each of the following numbers in full, not in standard form.

     (a) Ben Nevis is 1.343×10^3 m high.

     (b) Mercury is 5.8×10^7 km from the Sun.

     (c) The distance from the Earth to the nearest star is about 4.3×10^{13} km.

NM.5   A recipe for four people calls for $\frac{3}{4}$ teaspoonful of mustard powder. How much should I use for seven people?

NM.6   (a) Convert 20 m/s into km/h.

     (b) Convert 70 km/h into m/s.

Exercises	Statistics and measuring

SM.1   Which of the following are examples of continuous variables and which are discrete?

     ▸   Price of a loaf of bread in pence.

     ▸   Number of guillemots on a cliff face.

     ▸   Goals scored for and against a hockey team.

     ▸   Distance between major cities in miles.

     ▸   Air temperature at midday at a weather station in °C.

     ▸   Wind speed measured in kilometres per hour.

SM.2   Find the mean of each of the following batches of data.

     (a) 23   21   26   26   24

     (b) 101   107   98   92   115   102

The table below gives information on the number of brothers and sisters in a primary school class. Calculate the mean number of brothers and sisters of children in the class.

SM.3

Number of siblings	Frequency
0	7
1	18
2	5
3	2
4	0
5	1

Use computer software to produce a bar chart and a pie chart of these data.

Find the median, lower quartile and upper quartile of each of the following batches of data.

SM.4

(a) Here the batches of data have been sorted into ascending order.

    (i) 1.52 1.59 1.66 1.69 1.72 1.77

    (ii) 4 4 5 6 6 7 9 9 10

(b) Here the batches of data have not been sorted.

    (i) 31.50 23.70 71.00 33.55 27.40 43.90 51.80 63.20 72.45

    (ii) 22 83 56 24 35 61 53 54 29 92 74 85

Number and algebra Exercises

Solve the following equations.

NA.1

(a) $2x + 1 = 5$ (b) $\frac{1}{2}(x - 1) = 3$ (c) $12 = 5 + \frac{x}{21}$

Solve the following pairs of simultaneous equations.

NA.2

(a) $x - y = 2$ (b) $2x = y - 1$
    $2x - y = 7$ $3x = y + 1$

(c) $2y - x = 3$ (d) $3x - 3y = 3$
    $3x + 2y = 15$ $7x - 4y = 1$

In each of the following make x the subject of the formula.

NA.3

(a) $y = 2x + 1$ (b) $y = \frac{1}{2}x - 1$ (c) $y = 2(x + 1)$

NA.4   The graph of $y = 3x + 2$ is shown below.

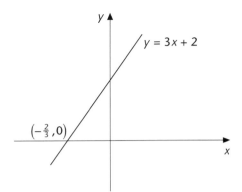

(a) Show that the point ($-\frac{2}{3}$, 0) lies on the line.

(b) Find the coordinates of the point where the line cuts the *y*-axis.

(c) Find the gradient of the line.

Exercises	Geometry and algebra

GA.1   For each angle you can find, decide whether it is acute, a right angle, obtuse, or reflex. The last figure has 12 different angles, not including ones which involve a full turn or more!

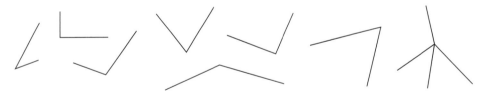

GA.2   The diagram below is made up of lines in three directions, each parallel set being marked with the same kind of arrows. There are two marked angles *a* and *b*. Label all of the remaining angles which are an *a* angle, a *b* angle or an *a* + *b* angle.

Hint: extend some lines so that they meet.

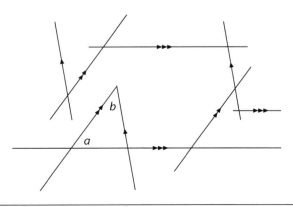

In the diagrams, find the sizes of all the marked angles. The additional lines in the second are each parallel to one line in the first.

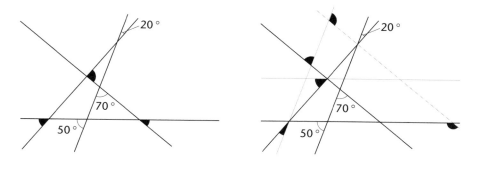

Give the coordinates of the four points on the grid shown. Use Pythagoras' theorem to find the distances between each pair of points. Use your results to verify that the figure is a square.

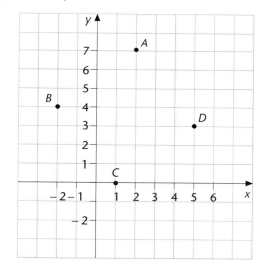

Using a pair of compasses and a device for finding the mid-point of a line segment, work out procedures for:

(a) drawing the triangle whose vertices are the mid-points of the edges of the triangle *ABC*;

(b) drawing a circle through the vertices of triangle *ABC* (suggestion: the centre of such a circle has to be equidistant from all three vertices, so consider two at a time);

(c) constructing the bisector of angle *A* (suggestion: draw a circle centred at the vertex of the angle, then two equi-radius circles with centres where the first circle cuts the arms of the triangle).

GA.6 — How many trapezia, parallelograms and triangles can you find in this diagram?

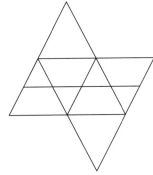

GA.7 — Which of the following are unchanged (invariant) by a translation?

Look at the translations in the tiling of triangles on page 103.

Lengths (distances between any two points).
Angles (between any two lines).
A line parallel to the direction of translation.
A line perpendicular to the direction of translation.

Exercises	Chance and reasoning

CR.1 — A card is selected from a pack of playing cards. What is the probability that it is:

(a)   a red ace;   (b)   a seven or an eight;   (c)   either an ace or a king?

CR.2 — A card is selected from a pack of playing cards. What is the probability that it is:

(a)   a heart or a six;   (b)   a king or a spade?

CR.3 — A card is selected from a pack of playing cards, and then replaced. Another card is drawn from the pack at random. Calculate the probability of getting:

(a)   two hearts;   (b)   two cards of the same suit.

Exercises	Proof and reasoning

PR.1 — (a) Prove the following statements using deductive arguments.

(i)   If m and n are both odd numbers, then $m + n$ is even.
(ii) If m and n are both even numbers, then $m + n$ is even.

(b) State and prove two statements which indicate whether the following are odd or even:

(i)   the product of two even numbers;
(ii) the product of two odd numbers.

Find counter-examples to disprove each of the following statements.

PR.2

(a) For any number n, $3n > 2n$.

(b) If $n > 0$ then $n^2 > n$.

(c) If $n > 0$ then $\dfrac{2}{n} < 2$.

(d) If $m \times n$ is even then m and n are both even.

Two equilateral triangles joined edge to edge form a diamond. Three triangles joined edge to edge form a triamond, four form a tetriamond and five a pentiamond.

PR.3

Prove, by exhaustion, that:

(a) there is exactly one triamond;

(b) there are exactly three tetriamonds;

(c) there are exactly four pentiamonds.

Assume each shape can be turned over.

(a) Egyptian fractions are fractions with numerator 1. In this system other fractions had to be expressed as the sum of Egyptian fractions, each one with a different denominator. Methods to find these expressions became quite ingenious.

PR.4

Look at (and perhaps check) the following fraction calculations:

$$\tfrac{2}{3} = \tfrac{1}{3} + \tfrac{1}{4} + \tfrac{1}{12} \qquad \tfrac{2}{5} = \tfrac{1}{5} + \tfrac{1}{6} + \tfrac{1}{30} \qquad \tfrac{2}{7} = \tfrac{1}{7} + \tfrac{1}{8} + \tfrac{1}{56}$$

Generalize from these examples to give an expression for $\dfrac{2}{2n-1}$ and prove that your expression works for all counting numbers n.

(b) Investigate what happens when the following sets of Egyptian fractions are added. Try to produce and prove a generalization from these special cases.

(i) $\tfrac{1}{4} + \tfrac{1}{5} + \tfrac{1}{20} =$ (ii) $\tfrac{1}{6} + \tfrac{1}{7} + \tfrac{1}{42} =$ (iii) $\tfrac{1}{8} + \tfrac{1}{9} + \tfrac{1}{72} =$

Solutions and notes

Solutions	Number and measure

NM.1
(a) (i) $\frac{40}{100} = \frac{2}{5}$ (ii) $\frac{8}{100} = \frac{2}{25}$ (iii) $\frac{70}{100} = \frac{7}{10}$ (iv) $\frac{67}{100}$

(b) (i) 0.5   (ii) 0.85   (iii) 0.07   (iv) 0.16

(c) (i) 80%   (ii) 21%   (iii) 240%   (iv) 50%

(v) $\frac{1}{8}$ = 0.125 = 12.5%   (vi) $\frac{1}{9}$ ≈ 0.111... ≈ 11.1%

NM.2
(a) 75% of 840 = 0.75 × 840 = 630, so 630 wives were in paid employment.

(b) 40% of 840 = 0.4 × 840 = 336, so 336 husbands earned over £18 000 a year.

(c) 18% of 840 = 0.18 × 840 = 151.2. But 151.2 is not a whole number. We'd probably say 151 or 152 couples had a joint income of less than £120 per week.

NM.3
(a) Light travels 9.4607×10^{12} km in a year.

(b) The distance from the centre of the Earth to the centre of the Moon is 3.844×10^5 km.

(c) Saturn is 1.427×10^9 km from the Sun.

(d) The mass of the Earth is 5.976×10^{24} kg.

(e) The Mediterranean Sea has an area of 2.504×10^6 km^2.

(f) Annapurna I is 8.091×10^3 m high.

NM.4
(a) Ben Nevis is 1343 m high.

(b) Mercury is 58 000 000 km from the Sun.

(c) The distance from the Earth to the nearest star is about 43 000 000 000 000 km.

NM.5
For four people I want $\frac{3}{4}$ teaspoonful. For one person I want $\frac{1}{4} \times \frac{3}{4}$ teaspoonful. For seven people I want $7 \times \frac{1}{4} \times \frac{3}{4} = \frac{21}{16} = 1\frac{5}{16}$ teaspoonfuls.

In practice I would not try to measure out $1\frac{5}{16}$ teaspoonfuls; I would use about $1\frac{1}{4}$ teaspoonfuls.

NM.6
(a) 20 metres per second means that, in one hour, 20 × 60 × 60 metres are travelled. (Check: you travel further in an hour than in a second.) So 20 m/s is equivalent to 72 000 m/h. To convert this to kilometres, divide by 1000, giving 72 km/h.

(b) 70 km/h is 70×1000 m/h, which in turn is $\frac{70 \times 1000}{60 \times 60} \approx 19.44$ m/s.

Notice that it is easier to carry out these conversions in two stages – convert the distance in one stage and the time in another stage – than to try to remember a formula for the conversion.

Statistics and measuring	Solutions

Discrete: prices, numbers of guillemots, goals.

Continuous: distances, air temperatures, wind speeds.

SM.1

(a) $\frac{120}{5} = 24$ (b) $\frac{615}{6} = 102.5$

SM.2

The mean number of brothers and sisters is $\frac{39}{33} \approx 1.2$.

SM.3

(a) (i) 1.52 <u>1.59</u> 1.66 | 1.69 <u>1.72</u> 1.77
median = 1.675, lower quartile = 1.59, upper quartile = 1.72

(ii) 4 4 | 5 6 <u>6</u> 7 9 | 9 10
median = 6, lower quartile = 4.5, upper quartile = 9

(b) (i) 23.70 27.40 | 31.50 33.55 <u>43.90</u> 51.80 63.20 | 71.00 72.45
median = 43.90, lower quartile = 29.45, upper quartile = 67.10

(ii) 22 24 29 | 35 53 54 | 56 61 74 | 83 85 92
median = 55, lower quartile = 32, upper quartile = 78.5

SM.4

Number and algebra	Solutions

(a) $x = 2$ (b) $x = 7$ (c) $x = 147$

NA.1

(a) $x = 5, y = 3$ (b) $x = 2, y = 5$

(c) $x = 3, y = 3$ (d) $x = {}^{-}1, y = {}^{-}2$

NA.2

(a) $x = \frac{1}{2}(y - 1)$ (b) $x = 2(y + 1)$ (c) $x = \frac{1}{2}y - 1$

NA.3

(a) $(^{-}\frac{2}{3}, 0)$ fits $y = 3x + 2$ because

$$3 \times (^{-}\tfrac{2}{3}) + 2 = {}^{-}2 + 2 = 0$$

(b) This is given by the intercept on the y-axis, and so is the point (0, 2).

(c) gradient $= \dfrac{\text{rise}}{\text{run}} = \dfrac{2 - 0}{0 - \left(^{-}\frac{2}{3}\right)} = \dfrac{2}{\frac{2}{3}} = 3$

NA.4

GA.1   Note that each angle is accompanied by another to make up a full turn.

Here *r* stands for reflex, *a* for acute, *o* for obtuse, and *p* for perpendicular (that is, right-angled). In the final figure just five of the many other angles made by combining adjacent angles together have been labelled.

GA.2   There are six *a* angles, six *b* angles, and six *a* + *b* angles (as well as others you may have created by joining up lines).

GA.3   Using the fact that a straight line is an angle of 180° and that the sum of the angles of a triangle is also 180°, the sizes of the marked angles can be found. The fact that the exterior angle of a triangle is the sum of the interior opposite angles can be used as well, as can the fact that vertically opposite angles are equal, but the first two facts are all that are needed.

The distance between A and B can be found by drawing in the right-angled triangle and seeing that the vertical height of the triangle is 4 and the horizontal width is 3, from which the hypotenuse is $\sqrt{3^2 + 4^2} = 5$.

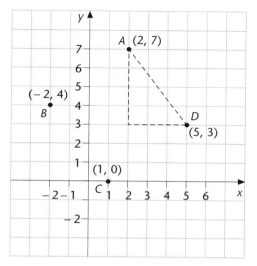

Similar calculations show that all the sides of the figure are the same length so it must be a rhombus. Calculating the length of a diagonal in a similar fashion shows it to be $\sqrt{7^2 + 1^2} = \sqrt{50}$ which is what you would get if the two edges of length 5 were at right angles. So they must indeed be at right angles.

(a) Note that the triangle of mid-points is scaled ('enlarged') by a factor of $\frac{1}{2}$ from the original triangle, and that its edges are parallel to the edges of the original triangle.

(b) To draw a circle through the vertices of the triangle, draw the perpendicular bisectors of two edges (all three are concurrent, that is, meet at the centre of the required circle).

(c) To bisect an angle, use the suggestion and the diagram to re-construct a construction. Why does the dashed line have to be the angle bisector?

There are 14 triangles, 15 parallelograms and 18 trapezia.

Translation does not change lengths and angles. A line in the direction of the translation will have its points translated to new points on the same line. A line perpendicular to the direction of a translation will be moved (unless the translation is by a distance of 0, in which case every point stays fixed).

Solutions	Chance and reasoning
CR.1	(a) $\dfrac{2}{52}$ (b) $\dfrac{8}{52}$ (c) $\dfrac{8}{52}$
CR.2	(a) $\dfrac{16}{52}$ (b) $\dfrac{16}{52}$
CR.3	(a) $\dfrac{1}{4} \times \dfrac{1}{4} = \dfrac{1}{16}$ (b) $P(\heartsuit\,\heartsuit) + P(\diamondsuit\,\diamondsuit) + P(\spadesuit\,\spadesuit) + P(\clubsuit\,\clubsuit) = \dfrac{1}{16} + \dfrac{1}{16} + \dfrac{1}{16} + \dfrac{1}{16} = \dfrac{4}{16} = \dfrac{1}{4}$

Solutions	Proof and reasoning
PR.1 See page 6. If p and q are positive whole numbers then so is $p + q - 1$. If a and b are positive whole numbers then so is $a + b$.	These proofs depend on the fact that even numbers can be written in the form $2k$ and odd numbers in the form $2k - 1$. (a) (i) Let $m = 2p - 1$ and $n = 2q - 1$, where $p \geq 1$ and $q \geq 1$. Then $m + n = 2p - 1 + 2q - 1 = 2(p + q - 1)$ which is an even number. (ii) Let $m = 2a$ and $n = 2b$ where $a \geq 1$ and $b \geq 1$. Then $m + n = 2a + 2b = 2(a + b)$ which is an even number. (b) In fact the product of two odd numbers is odd and the product of two even numbers is even. (i) If m and n are both odd numbers then $m \times n$ is odd. Let $m = 2p - 1$ and $n = 2q - 1$, where $p \geq 1$ and $q \geq 1$. Then $m \times n = (2p - 1)(2q - 1) = 4pq - 2p - 2q + 1$ $= 2(2pq - p - q) + 1$ which is an odd number. (ii) If m and n are both even numbers then $m \times n$ is even. Let $m = 2a$ and $n = 2b$ where $a \geq 1$ and $b \geq 1$. Then $m \times n = 2a \times 2b = 4ab = 2(2ab)$ which is an even number.
PR.2	(a) The statement would be true for $n > 0$ but any other values provide counter-examples. So for example, if $n = {}^-1$ then $3n = {}^-3$ and $2n = {}^-2$ so $3n < 2n$. (b) The statement would be true for $n > 1$, but not for numbers between 0 and 1. So for example, if $n = 0.5$, then $n^2 = 0.25$ and $n^2 < n$. (c) The statement would be true for $n > 1$, but not for numbers between 0 and 1. So for example, if $n = 0.5$, then $\dfrac{2}{n} = \dfrac{2}{0.5} = 4$ and so $\dfrac{2}{n} > 2$. (d) For example $m = 2$ and $n = 3$.

(a) In the diamond there are four free triangle sides. Placing a triangle on each of these in turn gives four cases all of which are identical to each other, so there is only one triamond.

PR.3

(b) In the triamond there are five free triangle sides. Placing a triangle on each of these in turn gives five cases. These give three different tetriamonds.

(c) In each tetriamond there are six free triangle sides. Placing a triangle on each of these in turn gives six cases. These give four different pentiamonds.

(a) If n is a whole number with $n \geq 2$ then $\dfrac{2}{2n-1} = \dfrac{1}{2n-1} + \dfrac{1}{2n} + \dfrac{1}{2n(2n-1)}$

PR.4

Proof

$$\frac{1}{2n-1} + \frac{1}{2n} + \frac{1}{2n(2n-1)} = \frac{2n}{2n(2n-1)} + \frac{2n-1}{2n(2n-1)} + \frac{1}{2n(2n-1)}$$

$$= \frac{2n + 2n - 1 + 1}{2n(2n-1)} = \frac{2 \times 2n}{2n \times (2n-1)} = \frac{2}{2n-1}$$

(b) (i) $\frac{1}{4} + \frac{1}{5} + \frac{1}{20} = \frac{5}{20} + \frac{4}{20} + \frac{1}{20} = \frac{10}{20} = \frac{1}{2}$

(ii) $\frac{1}{6} + \frac{1}{7} + \frac{1}{42} = \frac{7}{42} + \frac{6}{42} + \frac{1}{42} = \frac{14}{42} = \frac{1}{3}$

(iii) $\frac{1}{8} + \frac{1}{9} + \frac{1}{72} = \frac{9}{72} + \frac{8}{72} + \frac{1}{72} = \frac{18}{72} = \frac{1}{4}$

If n is a whole number with $n \geq 2$ then

$$\frac{1}{2n} + \frac{1}{2n+1} + \frac{1}{2n(2n+1)} = \frac{1}{n} \ .$$

Proof

$$\frac{1}{2n} + \frac{1}{2n+1} + \frac{1}{2n(2n+1)} = \frac{2n+1}{2n(2n+1)} + \frac{2n}{2n(2n+1)} + \frac{1}{2n(2n+1)}$$

$$= \frac{2n + 1 + 2n + 1}{2n(2n+1)} = \frac{2(2n+1)}{2n(2n+1)} = \frac{1}{n}$$

Guide to Assessing Your Mathematical Subject Knowledge and Understanding

PRIMARY INITIAL TEACHER TRAINING
A SUPPLEMENTARY SELF-EVALUATION GUIDE

Introduction

Welcome to the *Guide to Assessing Your Mathematical Subject Knowledge and Understanding* section, which is designed to help you get started on some mathematical work before the formal start of your Teacher Training course. If you have not studied for a while this will help you to get organized and will also help to reduce the amount of work to be done during the course.

Requirements

The Teacher Training Agency (TTA) requires that your current mathematical knowledge, understanding and skills are audited by your ITT provider against a TTA specification and that any gaps or misunderstandings are identified and rectified before the end of the course.

Mathematics GCSE grade C (or equivalent) is one of the qualifications required for acceptance on a training course leading to qualified teacher status (QTS). You may well feel therefore that the knowledge you have is sufficient to enable you to teach mathematics at Primary level. However, in order to teach effectively your knowledge and understanding needs to be sufficiently complete and relevant to meet the needs of the children you will be teaching, particularly in the following areas:

- number and algebra
- mathematical proof and reasoning
- measures
- shape and space
- probability and statistics.

The precise TTA requirements are specified in Department for Education and Employment (DfEE) Circular 4/98 Requirements for Courses of Initial Teacher Training Annex D Section C Trainees' Knowledge and Understanding of Mathematics. (This can be downloaded from http://www.teach-tta.gov.uk/itt/requirements/index.htm)

This is in *addition* to Annex D Sections A and B, although there is some overlap between the sections.

The curriculum for ITT is very full and you are therefore advised to start work on self-auditing your mathematical knowledge and understanding and working towards the required level before starting the course proper.

Needs assessment

This guide is designed to help you audit your current competence and suggest ways that you can overcome any deficiency using this book. If you are particularly concerned about aspects of your mathematics then you may also need a higher-level GCSE textbook or study guide to provide additional practice examples.

If you have particular difficulties, additional help may be available from your ITT provider either face-to-face or via electronic conferencing.

Using this guide

The remainder of this guide is in two sections:

1. 'Reviewing your current mathematical knowledge and understanding', which aims to help you identify any areas of weakness.

2. A 'Practice Assessment Test', which has an example of the type of questions you will need to be able to answer when your mathematics knowledge and understanding is formally assessed by your ITT provider.

In 'Reviewing your current mathematical knowledge and understanding' there are a series of activities for you to audit your current knowledge and understanding, which are also cross-referenced to previous sections of the book. You may find that there are topics of which you have little or no knowledge. This may be because you achieved your mathematics qualification some time ago, or the topic was not covered in the particular syllabus you followed.

For each activity you will be asked to assess your own competence and confidence. It is possible to get correct solutions without fully understanding! Only you can assess whether you are confident in applying your knowledge and skills. (A good strategy is, after you have tried all the questions, to go back through them and see if you think you could answer a different question 'like' that; then try to construct a testing question of the same sort of type. If you are in contact with a colleague, try exchanging questions.)

The 'Practice Assessment Test' is for you to use once you are confident in your mathematical knowledge and understanding. It is worth doing this under 'test conditions' to prepare yourself for the formal assessment which may be timed.

Reviewing your current mathematical knowledge and understanding

Using the audit questions to plan future work

You should work through all the audit questions, doing what you can (but without looking at the answers).

Check your answers, and as you do, note what you feel about each topic, perhaps decide a priority 1–5:

1. new to you – need to learn from scratch

2. something with which you recall having difficulties in the past

3. a bit rusty – need some practice

4. not a problem to do, but need to check on understanding

5. thoroughly familiar and fully understood.

You could do this in the margin on your working page. Once you have completed and marked the audit you can make a prioritised list of topics – doing this will enable you to make best use of the revision time you have available.

The solutions are cross-referenced to pages in the previous chapters to enable you to look up particular topics. However, if you find that you have a number of deficiencies within a mathematical topic it may be better to work through a whole section.

Once you are fully confident that your skills, knowledge and understanding are to the level required, then try the Practice Test.

Audit

Work through the following audit questions doing what you can without looking at the answers. Do not worry at this stage if something is unfamiliar, you cannot remember something you once knew, or you are just unsure: just go on to the next question. The purpose is to identify what you need to learn or revise in the next few weeks.

The real number system

1. Put the following numbers in numerical order as they would appear on a number line:

$\frac{1}{3}$, 3^2, $-\frac{1}{3}$, -0.3, 3^{-2}

2. Say whether each of the following four statements is true or false: correct as necessary.

(a) $0.2 \times -0.3 = 0.6$

(b) $\frac{4}{15} - \frac{7}{20} = -\frac{25}{300}$

(c) $1\frac{3}{4} \div 4\frac{2}{3} = \frac{21}{56}$

(d) $65 < 21$

3. Draw an outline number line which indicates all numbers between 17 and 35 (including 17 but not including 35).

4. Write the following in index notation:

(a)   10 000

(b)   0.001

5. (a)   Write 256.87 in standard form (scientific notation).

(b)   Write 0.0045 in standard form.

(c)   Write 0.5 the product of your previous two answers in standard form.

6. Take the number 31.567 and write to:

(a)   The nearest whole number.

(b)   Two decimal places.

(c)   One significant figure.

7. Write $\frac{1}{9}$ as a recurring decimal.

8. What type of number is $\frac{1}{4}$ when converted to a decimal?

9. Write 0.5 (i.e. 0.555...) as an exact fraction.

10. Why is (i.e. 0.3333...) a rational number?

11. Why is $\sqrt{2}$ an irrational number?

12. What type of number is π?

Number operations and algebra

13. On different calculators, the following key presses can produce different answers:

2 $\boxed{+}$ 3 $\boxed{\times}$ 4 $\boxed{=}$

A simple calculator gives the answer 20, but a scientific one gives 14. Explain how these answers occur.

14. Calculate each of the following, without using a calculator:

(a) $32 + 2 \times 5 + 6 =$

(b) $(32 + 2) \times 5 + 6 =$

(c) $(32 + 2) \times 5^2 + 6 =$

(d) $(20 + 7)(10 + 5) =$

(e) $\dfrac{27 \times 1.08 \times 6.4}{1.2 \times 7.2 \times 2.4} =$

15. Three people who share a house decide to split a £70 food bill between them, taking into account the number of meals eaten at home. They agree that it should be split in the ratio 2 to 3 to 5. How much does each person pay?

16. An article costing £300 is in a sale at £225. By what percentage has it been decreased?

17. What are the prime factors of 396?

18. Factorise the expression $5a^3b^2 + 5ab^3$.

19. Use the formula $C = \frac{5}{9}(F - 32)$ to calculate the Fahrenheit temperature equivalent to 15°C.

20. Which of the following expressions are equivalent?

    (a) $(3a - 3)(a - 1)$

    (b) $3a(a - 2) + 3$

    (c) $3a^2 - 6a + 3$

    (d) $3(a - 1)^2$

    (e) $3[a(a - 2) + 1]$

21. For the sequence of odd numbers 1, 3, 5, 7…

    (a) What are the next 3 numbers?

    (b) What is the nth term?

    (c) What is the sum of the first n terms?

Equations, functions and graphs

22. Calculate the number(s) that satisfy the following conditions:

    (a) Two more than a number is the square root of 9.

    (b) The sum of a number and its square is 12 more than its double.

    (c) The sum of two numbers is 5 and their product 6.

    (d) $3y = 2x + 7$ and $y = -2x + 1$

23. On a square grid, plot the points $(-2, -1)$ and $(1, 2)$ and draw a straight line passing through both points.

    (a) What is the y-intercept of the line?

    (b) What is the gradient of the line?

    (c) What is the equation of the line?

24. On the same grid as Q24, plot the graph of the function $y = -3x - 1$.

    (a) What is the y-intercept of this line?

    (b) What is the gradient of the line?

    (c) What are the co-ordinates of the point where the two lines intersect?

Mathematical reasoning and proof

25. What do the following symbols mean?

    (a) $=$

    (b) $\Rightarrow$

    (c) $\equiv$

    (d) $\therefore$

    (e) $\approx$

    (f) $\geq$

26. Prove or disprove the following using deductive proof, proof by exhaustion or counter-example as appropriate:

    (a) Numbers divisible by 9 are also divisible by 3.

    (b) Any quadrilateral with a pair of parallel sides is a parallelogram.

    (c) There are 11 possible totals from adding the numbers on two six-sided dice.

Measures

27. What are the Système Internationale (SI) prefix and the symbol for 10^6?

28. 1 UK gallon $\approx$ 4.55 litres.

    (a) If fuel costs 75p/litre, how much is this in £/gallon?

    (b) Convert 20 litres to gallons.

29. If a temperature is given as $50° \pm 5°$, what is the relative error for this reading?

30. A cube has a side of 2 cm:

    (a) What is the area of one face?

    (b) What is the volume?

31. On a map with a scale of 1:25 000 the distance between two places is 50 mm. What is the actual distance on the ground in kilometres?

Shape and space

32. What is a reflex angle?

33. Calculate all the angles in the following diagram:

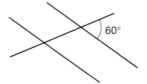

34. For each of the following shapes draw in all the line(s) of reflective symmetry:

(a)

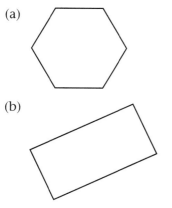

(b)

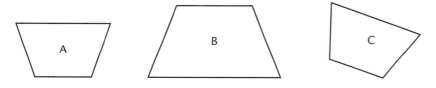

35. Which of these shapes are similar and which congruent?

36. How many times must a square be rotated through 90° in one direction to return to its original position?

37. What is the length of the hypotenuse of a right-angled triangle where the other two sides are 5 cm and 12 cm?

38. Give three properties of a rectangle involving

   (a) the sides

   (b) the angles

   (c) the diagonals.

39. What is the formula for the area of this trapezium?

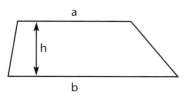

40. What is the area of a 3, 4, 5 right-angled triangle?

41. Draw the net of a 3, 4, 5 right-angled triangular prism that is 2 units long.

   (a) What is the volume of the above prism?

   (b) What is the total surface area of the prism?

42. The diagram shows a circle of radius 3 cm. The shaded sector is one third of the circle.

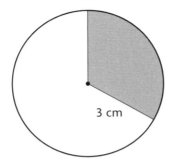

3 cm

(a) What is the area of the sector?

(b) What is the length of the perimeter of the sector?

43. A regular octahedron has 8 faces and 6 vertices; how many edges does it have?

44. What shape are the faces of a regular dodecahedron?

Probability and statistics

45. Explain the difference between a bar chart and a histogram.

46. What does the area of a pie chart represent?

47. Name the key features of the following boxplot (box and whisker diagram).

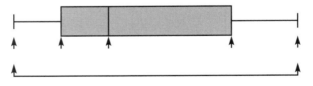

48. Using the data tabulated below calculate:

(a) the median

(b) the mode

(c) the mean.

Height h		Number	
$120 \leq h < 130$		9	
$130 \leq h < 140$		42	
$140 \leq h < 150$		69	
$150 \leq h < 160$		34	
$160 \leq h < 170$		6	

49. Draw a tree diagram showing the possible outcomes of throwing a six-sided die and then tossing a coin.

50. Explain the terms 'independent' and 'mutually exclusive' events.

Using solutions

As you check your solutions remember to decide a priority 1–5:

You could do this in the margin on your working page.

1. new to you – need to learn from scratch

2. something with which you recall having difficulties in the past

3. a bit rusty – need some practice

4. not a problem to do, but need to check on understanding

5. thoroughly familiar and fully understood.

Alongside each solution is a reference to the pages in the previous chapters where you can find help on that topic, for example [page 43]. Use these to plan your revision after you have marked the whole audit and assessed your needs.

Audit solutions

The real number system

1.

$-0.33...,$	-0.3	$0.11...$	$0.33...$	9
$-\frac{1}{3}$	-0.3	3^{-2} $(\frac{1}{3}^2 = \frac{1}{9})$	$\frac{1}{3}$	3^2

2. (a) $0.2 \times 0.3 = 0.6$ FALSE (-0.06) [page 35]

   (b) $\frac{4}{15} - \frac{7}{20} = -\frac{25}{300}$ TRUE but $-\frac{1}{12}$ a simpler solution. [page 15]

   (c) $1\frac{3}{4} \div 4\frac{2}{3} = \frac{21}{56}$ TRUE but $\frac{3}{8}$ is simpler. [pages 15, 34]

   (d) $65 < 21$ FALSE (65 is greater than 21). [page 88]

3. [page 88]

   17   35

4. (a) $10\ 000 = 10^4$ [page 19]

   (b) $0.001 = 10^{-3}$ [page 19]

5. (a) $256.87 = 2.5687 \times 10^2$ in standard form (scientific notation). [page 20]

   (b) $0.0045 = 4.5 \times 10^{-3}$ in standard form. [page 20]

   (c) 1.155915×10^0. [page 20]

6. (a) 31.567 = 32 to the nearest whole number.

   (b) 31.567 = 31.57 correct to 2 decimal places.

   (c) 31.567 = 30 correct to 1 significant figure.

7. $\frac{1}{9} = 0.\dot{1}$ (i.e. 0.1111... or 0.1 recurring). [page 17]

8. $\frac{1}{4} = 0.25$ which is a terminating decimal. [page 17]

9. $0.\dot{5} = \frac{5}{9}$. [page 17]

10. $0.\dot{3}$ is a rational number because it can be obtained by dividing two integers (1/3). [page 17]

11. √2 is an irrational number because it cannot be obtained by dividing two integers. [page 17]

12. π is an irrational number (22/7 is only an approximation). [page 17]

Number operations and algebra

13. With scientific calculators multiplication takes precedence over addition, so they give 2 + (3 × 4) = 14. Simple calculators perform operations in the order of input. [page 28]

14. (a) 32 + 2 × 5 + 6 = 48 (multiplication before addition).

   (b) (32 + 2) × 5 + 6 = 176 (brackets first).

   (c) $(32 + 2) \times 5^2 + 6 = 856$ (indices then brackets).

   (d) (20 + 7)(10 + 5) = 200 +70+100+35 = 405. [page 81]

   (e) $\frac{2.7 \times 1.08 \times 6.4}{1.2 \times 7.2 \times 2.4} = 0.9$ (the key here is to 'cancel').

15. £14, £21, £35 ($\frac{2}{10}$, $\frac{3}{10}$ and $\frac{5}{10}$ of £70). [page 36]

16. 25% $\left(\dfrac{\text{difference}}{\text{original}} \times 100 = \dfrac{75}{300} \times 100 \right)$. [page 38]

17. 396 = 2 × 2 × 3 × 3 × 11. [page 31]

18. $5a^3 b^2 + 5ab^3 = 5ab^2 (a^2 + b)$. [page 82]

19. 59°F (i.e $\frac{9}{5} \times 15 + 32$). [page 90]

20. All the expressions are equivalent to each other. [page 81]

21. (a) 9, 11, 13 are the next 3 numbers. [page 78]

   (b) The nth term is $2n - 1$. [page 78]

   (c) n^2 (The sum of the first 2 terms = 4 = 2^2;

       the sum of the first 3 terms = 9 = 3^2......).

Equations, functions and graphs

22. (a) $n = 1$.

   $(n + 2) = \sqrt{9}$, so $n = 3 - 2$ Note: by convention $\sqrt{9}$ indicates the positive root of 9. If you took it to mean both roots then you would have two answers: $n = 1$ and $n = -5$.   [page 83]

   (b) 4 and -3

   $(n + n^2 = 2n + 12$, so $n^2 - n - 12 = 0$.

   Therefore $(n - 4)(n + 3) = 0)$.   [page 81]

   (c) 2 and 3 $(a + b = 5, a \times b = 6)$.   [page 86]

   (d) $x = -\frac{1}{2}, y = 2$.   [page 86]

23.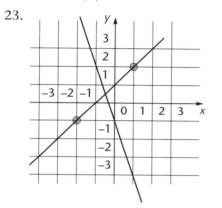

   (a) The y-intercept of the line is 1.

   (b) The gradient of the line is 1.

   (c) The equation of the line is $y = x + 1$.   [page 94]

24. (a) The y-intercept of $y = -3x - 1$ is -1.

   (b) The gradient of $y = -3x - 1$ is -3.

   (c) From the graph the point appears to be $(-\frac{1}{2}, -\frac{1}{2})$. Check whether this is so, by substituting in the equation of each line. At the point of intersection $y = -3x - 1$ and $y = x + 1$. Therefore,

   $-3x - 1 = x + 1$. Solve for x and substitute to find y. $(-\frac{1}{2}, -\frac{1}{2})$ is the point where the two lines intercept.   [page 94]

Mathematical reasoning and proof

25. (a) $=$ of the same value   [page 139]

   (b) $\Rightarrow$ implies that   [page 140]

   (c) $\equiv$ is always true   [page 139]

   (d) $\therefore$ therefore it follows that   [page 141]

   (e) $\approx$ approximately equal to

(f) ≥ greater than or equal to [page 88]

26. (a) Deductive proof: Let n be a number divided into k parts.
So, $n = 9k$
but $9 = 3 \times 3$
∴ $n = 3(3k)$, that is n is divisible by 3. [page 142]

(b) A trapezium has a pair of parallel sides but is not a parallelogram; so the statement is disproved by counter-example. [page 143]

(c) The 11 different scores are 2, 3, 4, 5, 6, 7, 8, 9, 10, 11, 12 as shown below:

	1	2	3	4	5	6
1	2	3	4	5	6	7
2	3	4	5	6	7	8
3	4	5	6	7	8	9
4	5	6	7	8	9	10
5	6	7	8	9	10	11
6	7	8	9	10	11	12

This is a proof by exhaustion. [page 145]

Measures

27. The SI prefix for 10^6 is 'mega' and the symbol M. [page 41]

28. (a) £3.41 to the nearest p (0.75×4.55).

(b) 4.40 gal (to 2 d.p.) (20 litres ≈ 20/4.55 gal). [page 47]

29. The relative error of 50° ± 5° is ±10%. [page 43]

30. (a) The area of one face of a cube of side 2 units is 4 cm^2.

(b) The volume of a cube of side 2 is 8 cm^3.

31. On a 1:25 000 map 50 mm represents 1.25 km on the ground.

Shape and space

32. A reflex angle is one which is greater than 180° but less than 360°.
[page 99–100]

33. The obtuse angles are 120°, the acute 60°.

34. (a) A regular hexagon has six lines of symmetry:

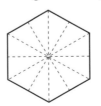

(b) A rectangle has two lines of symmetry:

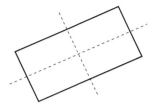

35. The shapes are all similar (equal angles and sides in proportion) but only A and C are congruent (same shape and same size). [page 109]

36. A square must be rotated 4 times through 90° in the same direction to return to its original position. [page 111]

37. Using Pythagoras' Theorem gives 13 ($\sqrt{(5^2 + 12^2)}$). [page 115]

38. (a) Both pairs of opposite sides are equal in length and parallel.

    (b) There are four equal angles which are right-angles.

    (c) Both diagonals are equal and bisect each other. [page 113]

39. The formula for the area of a trapezium is $\frac{1}{2}(a+b)h$. [page 118]

40. 6 sq units ($\frac{1}{2} \times 3 \times 4$).

41. Draw the net of a 3, 4, 5 right-angled triangular prism 2 units long.

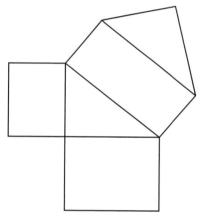

(There are other possible nets)

    (a) The volume of the above prism is 12 cu units (cross-section area × length).

    (b) The total surface area of the prism is 36 sq units.
    i.e. $(2 \times 6) + (2 \times 3) + (2 \times 4) + (2 \times 5)$.

42. (a) The area of a sector of a third of a circle with radius 3 cm is 9.42 sq units to 2 d.p. (i.e. $\frac{1}{3} \times \pi \times 3 \times 3$). [page 120]

    (b) The length of the perimeter of the sector above is 12.28 units (i.e. $3 + 3 + 2\pi \times \frac{3}{3}$).

43. An octahedron has 12 edges (Euler's relationship F + V = E + 2). [page 123]

44. The faces of a regular dodecahedron are regular pentagons. [page 122]

Probability and statistics

45. A bar chart is used for discrete data but a histogram is used for continuous data. [page 58–59]

46. The area of a pie chart represents the sample size – all the values of the sample together. [page 66]

47. Key features of a boxplot.

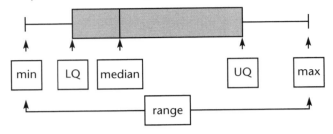

LQ – lower quartile, UQ – upper quartile. [page 63]

48.

Height h	Class mid-point	Number	
$120 \leq h < 130$	125	9	1125
$130 \leq h < 140$	135	42	5670
$140 \leq h < 150$	145	69	10005
$150 \leq h < 160$	155	34	5270
$160 \leq h < 170$	165	6	990
Totals		160	23060

(a) The median lies between 80 and 81 in rank order, so is in the 140–150 class.

(b) The mode is the class interval with the greatest number, so the mode is also 140–150.

(c) The mean = 23060/160 = 144.125. [page 60]

49. A tree diagram showing the possible outcomes of throwing a six-sided die and then tossing a coin (there are 12 possible outcomes).   [page 129]

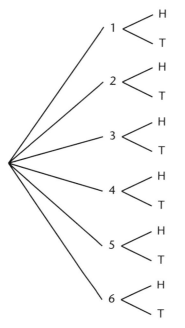

50. If two events are said to be 'independent' the chance of one occurring is unaffected by whether or not the other has occurred. For example, the events 'rolling a six' and 'tossing a head' are independent. Two events are said to be mutually exclusive if the occurrence of one excludes the possibility of the other occurring. For example, if a dice is rolled once, the events 'getting a 5' and 'getting an even score' are mutually exclusive.   [pages 130–131]

What now?

1. Think about those questions that you may have missed out of the audit. Has seeing the solutions reminded you about the topic? If so, a little revision may be enough. If not, perhaps the topic is not one you have studied before – most likely if you sat an intermediate rather than a higher paper.

2. What about questions where your answer was not right or not sufficiently complete? Was it a careless mistake or an underlying lack of understanding?

3. What about the questions you did get right? How convinced are you that you could answer any question on that topic? Were you relying on memory rather than understanding? Could you apply your skills, knowledge and understanding to more complex examples?

You should now make a list of topics that you need to:

▌ learn from scratch

▌ relearn

▌ revise

▌ practise a bit more.

Audit question no.	Topic	Page(s)	Priority	When to do	Completed

What next?

Revise and practise the topics you need to improve – how you order your priorities is up to you. To help keep up your morale, it might be sensible to alternate a topic which just needs 'brushing-up' with one that needs more work.

Once you are reasonably confident in all the topics, try the Practice Test in the next section. These questions require you to apply your skills, knowledge and understanding.

Practice assessment test

Purpose

Sometime during your teacher training course you will need to provide evidence that your mathematics subject knowledge and understanding are to the required TTA standard. You will probably have to do this by satisfactorily completing a test under examination conditions. The following test includes examples of the types of question you might be expected to answer. Use it both for examination practice and to familiarise yourself with questions which require you to apply your knowledge and understanding.

Part A comprises examples of calculations and statements that are not correct in some way. You need to correct or complete the answer, and say what misconception caused the error. Part B has examples of longer questions involving several topics.

Set aside at least an hour to work through all the questions. If you have any problems, leave those questions and come back to them at the end. Only look at the solutions once you have done as much as possible on the whole test.

Part A

Correct or amend the following:

1. 'Multiplication makes bigger.'

2. 'Subtraction makes smaller.'

3. '$0.3 \times -0.3 = 0.9$.'

4. '$52.3 \times 10 = 52.30$.'

5. '$\pi = 22/7$.'

6. '$123456789 = 12.3 \times 10^7$ in standard form correct to 3 significant figures.'

7. '$3^{-2} = -9$.'

8. '$\frac{1}{4} + \frac{2}{5} = \frac{3}{9}$.'

9. 'The following are equivalent to $\frac{1}{5}$:
   $\frac{3}{15}$; 25%; two tenths; 0.5.'

10. 'To find the original cost of an item reduced by 15% to £850:
    £850 × 15/100 = £127.50. £850 + £127.50 = £977.50.'

11. 'Congruent triangles are not similar.'

12. 'A right-angled triangle with sides of 3 and 4 must have the third side length 5.'

13. 'Scaling a shape by a factor of 2 doubles the perimeter and area.'

14. 'Discrete data must be whole numbers.'

15. 'If I throw a fair six-sided dice 60 times I will get 10 ones.'

Part B

16. The following data shows the result of an experiment to test reaction times of a group of people before and after some training. Represent this data graphically in a way that enables you to compare the two sets of results.

Person	Before	After
A	34	28
B	37	29
C	39	29
D	41	30
E	41	31
F	43	33
G	45	35
H	54	36
I	67	39
J	78	41

What is the average reaction time before training? after training?

(Use both median and mean and explain why mode does not apply here.)

Compare the ranges. How would you explain the differences you have found?

17. Look at the following pattern:

$3 + 1 = 4$

$5 + 3 + 1 = 9$

$7 + 5 + 3 + 1 = 16$

What is the next line?

What is the nth line?

18. There are two numbers a and b. When you add them together you get 25. When you subtract one from the other you get 11. What are a and b?

19. Calculate the point of intersection of the graphs of the equations $y = x + 4$ and $y = -2x + 5$. Which is the steeper of these two graphs? Explain your reasoning.

20. On a square grid mark points A (2,1) and B (1,2). Rotate each point 90° anti-clockwise around the origin, resulting in points C and D respectively.

   (a) Name the resulting shape ABCD. Calculate the area and perimeter of the shape ABCD.

   (b) How many lines of symmetry does it have?

   (c) Imagine that this shape is the cross-section of a solid metal bar of length 5 units. What volume of metal is there in the bar?

   (d) How many planes of symmetry does the bar have?

21. Imagine you are playing a game for 2 players which involves tossing a dice and a coin. You win if you get a six or a head. Otherwise your partner wins.

   (a) Show the possible outcomes on a tree diagram.

   (b) Is the game fair?

   (c) Are the events 'tossing a head' and 'winning' mutually exclusive?

22. Prove or disprove the following:

   (a) If a shape is a kite and it also has sides of equal length then it must be a square.

   (b) If a number is divisible by 12 then it is divisible by 3.

Solutions to practice test

As you check your solutions make some notes for yourself to indicate whether your solution was:

(a) correct and complete

(b) correct but missing some detail; for example, units or number of decimal places

(c) incorrect due to a careless error

(d) incorrect due to some misunderstanding

(e) missing.

Part A

For convenience, the question is repeated.

1. 'Multiplication makes bigger.'

   Not always, multiplication by a fraction makes smaller.

2. 'Subtraction makes smaller.'

   Not always, subtraction of a negative number makes larger.

3. '0.3 × –0.3 = 0.9.'

    $0.3 \times -0.3 = -0.09$

4. '52.3 × 10 = 52.30.'

    523.0

5. '$\pi = 22/7$.'

    No, this is an approximation. π is an irrational number so cannot be written exactly as a fraction.

6. '123456789 = 12.3×10^7 in standard form correct to 3 significant figures'

    1.23×10^8 correct to 3 significant figures (in standard form the number must be between 1 and 10).

7. '$3^{-2} = -9$'.
    $3^{-2} = (\frac{1}{3})^2 = \frac{1}{9} = $ (i.e. 0.1111...).

8. '$\frac{1}{4} + \frac{2}{5} = \frac{3}{9}$'.
    $\frac{1}{4} + \frac{2}{5} = \frac{5}{20} + \frac{8}{20} = \frac{13}{20}$

9. 'The following are equivalent to $\frac{1}{5}$: $\frac{3}{15}$; 25%; two tenths; 0.5.'
    $\frac{3}{15} = \frac{1}{5}$; 25% $= \frac{25}{100} = \frac{1}{4}$; $\frac{2}{10} = \frac{1}{5}$; $0.5 = \frac{5}{10} = \frac{1}{2}$

10. 'To find the original cost of an item reduced by 15% to £850. £850 × 15/100 = £127.50. £850 + £127.50 = £977.50'

    85%   of original price   = £850
             original price   = £850 × 100/85
             original price   =£1000

11. 'Congruent triangles are not similar.'

    Yes they are. ('Similar' shapes have the same shape but may differ in size. Congruent triangles are identical in size and shape; they are a special kind of similar triangles.)

12. 'A right-angled triangle with sides of 3 and 4 must have the third side length 5.'

    No, only if the side of length 4 is NOT the hypotenuse.

13. 'Scaling a shape by a factor of 2 doubles the perimeter and area.'

    The perimeter doubles but the area quadruples.

14. 'Discrete data must be whole numbers.'

    No, discrete data are in categories so can be names or numbers (e.g. colours or shoe sizes).

15. 'If I throw a fair six-sided dice 60 times I will get 10 ones.'

    Unlikely. The actual number could be anything between 0 and 60; 10 would be the average over a very large number of throws.

Part B

16. The following data shows the result of an experiment to test reaction times of a group of people before and after some training. Represent this data graphically in a way that enables you to compare the two sets of results.

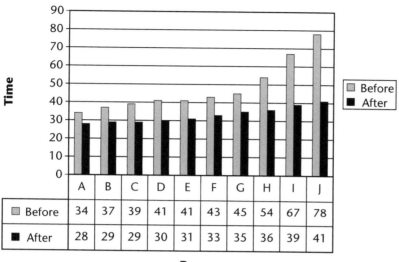

Reaction Times

Person	A	B	C	D	E	F	G	H	I	J
☐ Before	34	37	39	41	41	43	45	54	67	78
■ After	28	29	29	30	31	33	35	36	39	41

Note: The data does not have to be shown on the compound bar chart as above. Also note the convention of gaps between bar chart columns for discrete data (in this case each person is a 'discrete' category).

What is the average reaction time before training? after training?

(Use both median and mean and explain why mode does not apply here.)

	Before training	After training
Mean	47.9 (to 1 d.p.)	33.1 (to 1 d.p.)
Median	42	32
Range	44	13

Mode is not an appropriate summary measure. This data is a comparison of individual changes in reaction time – each result is only recorded once so the most frequent time is meaningless.

Compare the ranges. How would you explain the differences you have found?

Training reduces reaction time. It has greatest effect on those with the slowest initial reaction times, i.e. the least 'fit'.

17. Look at the following pattern:

$3 + 1 = 4$

$5 + 3 + 1 = 9$

$7 + 5 + 3 + 1 = 16$

What is the next line?

$9 + 7 + 5 + 3 + 1 = 25$

What is the nth line?

$(2n + 1) + (2n - 1) +... 5 + 3 + 1 = (n + 1)^2$

18. There are two numbers a and b. When you add them together you get 25. When you subtract one from the other you get 11. What are a and b?

$a + b = 25$
$a - b = 11$

adding

$2a = 36$
so $a = 18$

substituting 18 for a
$18 + b = 25$
so $b = 7$

19. Calculate the point of intersection of the graphs of the equations $y = x + 4$ and $y = -2x + 5$.

At the point of intersection:
$x + 4 = -2x + 5$
$3x + 4 = 5$
$3x = 1$
$x = \frac{1}{3}$
$y = \frac{1}{3} + 4$
$y = 4\frac{1}{3}$

Which is the steeper of these two graphs? Explain your reasoning.

$y = -2x + 5$. In the general expression for a straight line $y = mx + c$, m is the gradient. Although -2 is a negative gradient the line is steeper than $y = x + 4$ which has a gradient of 1.

20. On a square grid mark points A (2,1) and B (1,2). Rotate each point 90° anti-clockwise around the origin, resulting in points C and D.

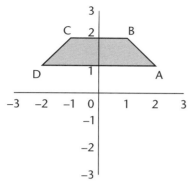

(a) Name the resulting shape ABCD:

Trapezium.

Calculate the area and perimeter of the shape ABCD:

Area = 1 × (2 + 4)/2 = 3 sq units
(half the sum of parallel sides × height).
Perimeter = AB + BC + CD + DA
$AB^2 = 1^2 + 1^2 = 2$ (Pythagoras) so AB = √2, CD also = √2
Perimeter = √2 + 2 + √2 + 4 units = 8.83 units
(correct to 2 decimal places).

(b) How many lines of symmetry does it have?

One (from midpoint BC to midpoint AD).

(c) Imagine that this shape is the cross-section of a solid metal bar of length 5 units. What volume of metal is there in the bar?

15 cu units (Area of cross-section × length).

(d) How many planes of symmetry does the bar have?

Two.

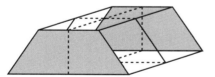

21. Imagine you are playing a game for 2 players which involves tossing a dice and a coin. You win if you get a six or a head. Otherwise your partner wins.

(a) Show the possible outcomes on a tree diagram.

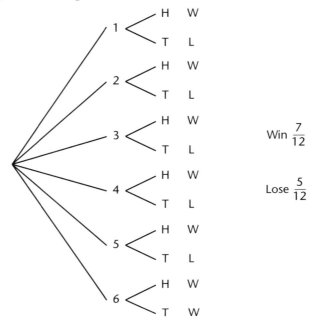

Win $\frac{7}{12}$

Lose $\frac{5}{12}$

(b) Is the game fair?

No, since it is possible for your partner to win in more than half of the possibilities.

(c) Are the events 'tossing a head' and 'winning' mutually exclusive?

No – it is possible to do both.

22. Prove or disprove the following:

(a) If a shape is a kite and it also has sides of equal length then it must be a square.

Disproved by counter-example: a rhombus has sides of equal length but is not a square.

(b) If a number is divisible by 12 then it is divisible by 3.

Deductive proof:

Let n be any number divisible by 12.
Then $n = 12k$ where k is a whole number
But $12k = 3 \times 4k$ which is divisible by 3 so n is divisible by 3.

Now what?

How did you get on with the Practice Test? How long did it take to complete?

Knowing particular mathematical facts and techniques is not the same as being able to apply these in differing contexts. You may have found that your understanding is not yet sufficiently secure.

Work through the solutions to any question with which you had major problems. Note which topics were problematic, and work through the relevant section of the book (the index or contents will help you to find the right sections). There is a Practice Exercises Section with worked solutions that may also help. Once you have done that try the question again. If you are still having problems you may need to acquire a GCSE higher-level textbook to get additional help and practice questions.

You should have been able to complete the test in 1 to $1\frac{1}{2}$ hours – if it took much longer you need to think about why that might have been. It may be some time since you did a mathematics examination and you need to gain more practice.

Once you have checked up on all areas of the mathematical knowledge needed to meet the ITT requirements, think carefully about whether you are ready to provide evidence of your understanding. A good strategy for doing this is to go back through the audit and practice questions to see if you think you could answer different questions 'like' that; then try to construct testing questions for yourself of the same sort of type. If you are in contact with a colleague, try exchanging questions.

Acknowledgements

Thank you to Sue Johnston-Wilder for supplying many of the practice test questions, and the Open University PGCE students who used them.

Mathematical dictionary

Throughout this book key terms are introduced in **bold** face. These are listed in the index below together with other important items.

Index

Developing a personalized mathematical dictionary

The index above gives page references to many of the mathematical terms used in this book. However, neither the selection of words nor the detail given is likely to be a perfect match for your own needs. Consequently, we urge you to start creating your own mathematical dictionary. This will give entries that are useful to you personally and, in addition, you will benefit from expressing the ideas in your own words.

Alternatively you may wish to create your dictionary electronically using a word-processing package. That way you can rearrange your entries at any stage and only print them out when you are ready.

We suggest that you use sheets of A4 writing paper or a notebook to make entries to your dictionary. As you work through the book pick out any words or phrases which are themselves unfamiliar or which are being used in an unfamiliar way. Write them down then make notes (which might include diagrams) about what you understand by them and add clear page references to remind you where they appear in the book. Leave some space after each entry in case you wish to add further information later as your understanding of a particular idea grows.

You may also wish to reserve a section of your dictionary for mathematical symbols and notation.